A Russian European: Paul Miliukov in Russian Politics. Thomas Riha.

A Search for Stability: U. S. Diplomacy Toward Nicaragua, 1925–1933. William Kamman.

Freedom and Authority in the West. George N. Shuster, ed.

Theory and Practice: History of a Concept from Aristotle to Marx. Nicholas Lobkowicz.

Coexistence: Communism and Its Practice in Bologna, 1945–1965. Robert H. Evans.

Marx and the Western World. Nicholas Lobkowicz, ed.

Argentina's Foreign Policy 1930–1962. Alberto A. Conil Paz and Gustavo E. Ferrari.

Italy after Fascism, A Political History, 1943–1965. Giuseppe Mammarella.

The Volunteer Army and Allied Intervention in South Russia 1917–1921. George A. Brinkley.

Peru and the United States, 1900–1962. James C. Carey.

Empire by Treaty: Britain and the Middle East in the Twentieth Century. M. A. Fitzsimons.

The USSR and the UN's Economic and Social Activities. Harold Karan Jacobson.

Chile and the United States: 1880–1962. Fredrick B. Pike.

East Central Europe and the World: Developments in the Post-Stalin Era. Stephen D. Kertesz, ed.

Soviet Policy Toward International Control and Atomic Energy. Joseph L. Nogee.

INTERNATIONAL STUDIES OF THE

COMMITTEE ON INTERNATIONAL RELATIONS

UNIVERSITY OF NOTRE DAME

The Russian Revolution and Religion, 1917–1925. Edited and translated by Bolesław Szcześniak.

Soviet Policy Toward the Baltic States, 1918–1940. Albert N. Tarulis.

Introduction to Modern Politics. Ferdinand Hermens.

Freedom and Reform in Latin America. Fredrick B. Pike, ed.

What America Stands For. Stephen D. Kertesz and M. A. Fitzsimons, eds.

The Representative Republic. Ferdinand Hermens.

Theoretical Aspects of International Relations. William T. R. Fox, ed.

Catholicism, Nationalism and Democracy in Argentina. John J. Kennedy.

Christian Democracy in Western Europe, 1820–1953. Michael P. Fogarty.

The Fate of East Central Europe. Stephen D. Kertesz, ed.

German Protestants Face the Social Question. William O. Shanahan.

Soviet Imperialism: Its Origins and Tactics. Waldemar Gurian, ed.

The Foreign Policy of the British Labour Government, 1945–1951. M. A. Fitzsimons.

Diplomacy in a Whirlpool: Hungary between Nazi Germany and Soviet Russia. Stephen D. Kertesz.

Bolshevism: An Introduction to Soviet Communism. Waldemar Gurian.

*The Major Works of
Peter Chaadaev*

Peter Yakovlevich Chaadaev (1794–1856)

The Major Works of
Peter Chaadaev

A TRANSLATION AND COMMENTARY

RAYMOND T. McNALLY

Introduced by
RICHARD PIPES

UNIVERSITY OF NOTRE DAME PRESS
Notre Dame   London
1969

Grateful acknowledgment is made to the *Russian Review* for permission to use parts of Raymond McNally's article "The Significance of Chaadaev's *Weltanschauung*," which appeared in Volume 3, Number 4 (October, 1964).

Library of Congress Catalog Card Number: 68-20437
Manufactured in the United States of America

TO RITA

my firebrand
For whom my love and admiration grow stronger each day

Preface

PETER CHAADAEV emerges from the pages of Russian history as one of Russia's most provocative and influential thinkers. The purpose of this book is to present the reader with the first complete English translation of his major works. During the first half of the nineteenth century Chaadaev incited a violent polemic concerning the historical significance of Russian culture. His ideas concerning Russia's real mission in the world still provoke controversy in the Soviet Union. Yet, despite his significance, no complete English translation of his two major works, *The Philosophical Letters Addressed to a Lady* and *Apologia of a Madman,* has been published until now. My English translation with commentary and explanatory notes was done in the conviction that these materials should be made readily available to the English-reading public.

The background material in this book is expository; I have not attempted to write a complete biographical study of Chaadaev, nor have I tried to make any original inquiry into Chaadaev's philosophy. The point of view is simply that of a historian who admires Chaadaev's insights into the meaning of history in general and Russian history in particular, so the background material has been limited to a biographical sketch of Chaadaev and a short analysis of his major ideas on history. Since there was no definitive edition of Chaadaev's original works in print when this project was begun in 1961, a thorough search was made in the manuscript collections of Moscow and Leningrad. All the extant manuscripts of *The Philosophical Letters* and the *Apologia of a Madman* were found, studied, and evaluated to determine as far as possible how Chaadaev himself would have wanted these works to have appeared in print had he been able to publish all the *Letters* and the *Apologia* around 1836.

Utilizing the latest Soviet archival reference works, I was able to pinpoint the whereabouts of some of the Chaadaeviana. The manuscript collections in the Soviet Union provided me with further ·clues to other source materials. Having found the manuscripts, I had them microfilmed and began submitting them to tests to determine authenticity and relative reliability. I also tried to discover when each of the manuscripts had been written. I then concerned myself with the variants. In dealing with the manuscripts in which Chaadaev deleted whole passages and changed the wording of the texts himself, I used two criteria: 1) What changes apparently represented Chaadaev's final choices around October of 1836? 2) If Chaadaev had had the opportunity of preparing all *The Philosophical Letters* for publication in a completed series and the *Apologia of a Madman* around the end of 1836, which of the variants would he, in all likelihood, have chosen? The admirable scholarly work done on the Chaadaev manuscripts by the late Dmitri Ivanovich Shakhovskoi was of invaluable aid to me in completing this work. The result, my critical edition of the original manuscripts of Chaadaev's *Philosophical Letters* and *Apologia of a Madman,* was published in Berlin in 1966.

Having reconstructed the original texts by collating the various manuscripts, I translated them into English, to make Chaadaev accessible to students without a mastery of the French language. (Chaadaev wrote these works in French, rather than in Russian.) I have tried to concentrate upon the meaning, rather than the words, which Chaadaev was, in my opinion, attempting to communicate to the reader. In addition, despite the fact that the English-reading public is not accustomed to long periodic sentences in our day, I have almost invariably allowed them to stand as they appear in the manuscripts in order to convey some of the flavor of Chaadaev's style.

A word of warning seems in order here before this study begins: Chaadaev does not appeal to anyone in search of a systematized, unified philosophical analysis of history. He did not contribute anything particularly original to the academic field of philosophy or to that of history. His significance rests upon his peculiar application of a particular set of religious and philosophical ideas to the study of Russia's place in history. In Chaadaev's mind, the particular problem of the historical significance of Russian culture revolved around a few specific questions which he formulated for the first time, and in a highly provocative manner: Does Russia belong to the East or to the West? Is Russian culture European or Asiatic? Does it belong to the Judaeo-Christian, Graeco-Roman world? What historical role have Russians played in the past? Have they contributed anything original to world culture? What should Russia's mission be in the present and in the future?

I have already published the following articles on the development of some of Chaadaev's historical views: "Chaadaev's Evaluation of Peter the Great," *Slavic Review,* Vol. XXIII, No. 1 (March, 1964), pp. 31–44; "The Significance of Chaadaev's *Weltenschauung,*" *The Russian Review,* Vol. 3, No. 4 (October, 1964), pp. 352–361; "The Books in Petr Ja. Čaadaev's Libraries," *Jahrbücher fur Geschichte Osteuropas* Vol. XIV, No. 4 (December, 1966), pp. 495–512; "Chaadaev's Evaluation of Western Christian Churches," *The Slavonic and East European Review,* Vol. XLII, No. 99 (June, 1964), pp. 370–387; "Chaadaev Versus Xomjakov in the late 1830's and the 1840's," *Journal of the History of Ideas,* Vol. XXVII, No. 1 (January–March), 1966, pp. 73–91.

Acknowledgement is made to the Russian Research Center of Harvard University for arranging my use of the rich resources at the Widener Library. The Inter-University Committee on Travel Grants was generous in arranging a six-month stay in Russia. The American Philosophical Society (Penrose Fund) provided financial aid for microfilming and photostating source materials in Leningrad and Moscow, and the Academy of Sciences of the U.S.S.R. kindly permitted access to the source materials. Professor Richard Pipes of Harvard University was especially kind in providing help and advice at all stages in the preparation of this book, and I am particularly grateful to him. Professor Stephen Kertesz of the University of Notre Dame kindly took an interest in my work at an important point in my life, and helped me to persevere in my research.

The greatest debt of all I owe to my wife Rita to whom I have dedicated this book.

R.T.M.

Boston College

1968

Introduction

IN THE LUMINOUS intellectual atmosphere of Romantic Russia, the detached, melancholy figure of Chaadaev occupies a unique place. A friend of the Decembrists, he did not involve himself in their plot. An active member of the salons of the 1830's and 1840's, he stood aloof from their ideological alignments: a Schellingian, he did not join Odoevsky's circle devoted to the study of Schelling; a scathing critic of Russia's past, he did not belong to the Westerners; a deeply religious man, he was not one of the Slavophiles. Although Herzen placed him in the pantheon of martyrs for Russian liberty, Chaadaev did not really belong to any current or movement. He stands utterly alone in the history of Russian thought, a fascinating exception to almost any generalization that can be made about it.

Unlike other Russian intellectuals, Chaadaev did not concern himself with public affairs, with the people, with social improvement. He was preoccupied with the salvation of his soul. It is only because in Russia, where no politics is allowed, everything assumes a political significance, that he had been placed in the tradition of *obshchestvennaia mysl'*, that peculiar combination of public concerns and personal idealism. A true son of the Restoration Era, he longed for Christian unity and found life unbearably difficult in a country which, having drawn its Christianity from what he considered a poisoned source, had placed itself outside the mainstream of Divine history. No other major Russian thinker gave the counsel that he did in answer to the perennial question "what is to be done?": create a quiet preserve of inner peace and withdraw from an active life even while outwardly participating in it. The *Philosophical Letters,* his only major work, is permeated with the deepest kind of pessimism.

Professor McNally, who has previously brought out the first complete version of the *Philosophical Letters* in the original French, here undertakes the first full English translation of this difficult text. It is to be hoped that this edition will make a major Russian thinker of the Restoration Era better known among Western readers.

Harvard University   Richard Pipes

Contents

PREFACE   xi

INTRODUCTION   xvii

BIOGRAPHICAL SKETCH   1

SHORT ANALYSIS OF CHAADAEV'S
MAJOR IDEAS ON HISTORY   13

THE PHILOSOPHICAL LETTERS
ADDRESSED TO A LADY   21

    Letter I   23

    Letter II   52

    Letter III   72

    Letter IV   89

    Letter V   105

    Letter VI   124

    Letter VII   162

    Letter VIII   189

THE APOLOGIA OF A MADMAN   199

NOTES TO THE BIOGRAPHICAL SKETCH   221

NOTES TO THE ANALYSIS OF IDEAS   228

EXPLANATORY NOTES TO THE
PHILOSOPHICAL LETTERS   233

EXPLANATORY NOTES TO THE
APOLOGIA OF A MADMAN   252

INDEX   257

Wie schwer sind nicht die Mittel zu erwerben,
Durch die man zu den Quellen steigt!
Und eh' man nur den halben Weg erreicht,
Muss wohl ein armer Teufel sterben.

Faust. Part I

Biographical Sketch

In 1836 THE Moscow journal *Telescope* published Peter Chaadaev's "First Philosophical Letter." Chaadaev had written it as the introduction to his highly critical evaluation of Russian history and culture. The government immediately ordered the confiscation of all copies of the journal in which Chaadaev's article appeared. The tsarist officials exiled the editor to Siberia, dismissed the censor from his post, forbade even the mention of Chaadaev's name in the daily press, and extracted a promise from the author that he would never try to publish anything again. The tsar chose a singular method to deal with Chaadaev. Rather than send him into the usual Siberian exile, the tsar proclaimed that Chaadaev was officially insane! Chaadaev, until then a comparatively unknown drawing-room philosopher, became the "notorious" author of a work which the government considered dangerous enough to suppress. Immediately the journal containing his article was in great demand by local bookdealers who were not averse to selling proscribed literature under the counter. Many Russians reasoned that if the work was worth repressing, it had to be worth reading. Hundreds of

1

copies of Chaadaev's suppressed "First Philosophical Letter" were made by hand and circulated in manuscript form throughout the salons of Petersburg and Moscow. Chaadaev's article generated a violent polemic among his contemporary Russian intellectuals.

But the true irony of the so-called *"Telescope* Affair" lay less in the overt events themselves that in the fact that Chaadaev was never able to publish the rest of his works which would have clarified the nuances of his intellectual convictions. His "First Philosophical Letter" had been designed merely as a provocative beginning of a long work, entitled *Philosophical Letters Addressed to a Lady,* containing eight letters in all. Furthermore, the "First Philosophical Letter," though published in 1836, represented Chaadaev's initial point of view around 1829, when he had written it. But from 1829 to 1836 Chaadaev had undergone an evolution in thinking which was to culminate in the *Apologia of a Madman.* In order to understand the background of Chaadaev's statements in these major works of his, it is necessary to look into the important events in his lifetime, a lifetime filled with many changes of mind in reaction to a rapidly changing world.[1]

Peter Yakovlevich Chaadaev was born around the year 1794 either in Moscow or in the Nizhni-Novgorod region.[2] His family belonged to the Russian gentry. Most of his forefathers had been officers or administrators in the tsarist regime. Peter's mother was the daughter of Prince Mikhail M. Shcherbatov, the famous historian. The Shcherbatovs could trace their lineage back to old Kievan times.[3] Peter's father died in 1795 and his mother in 1797.[4] An unmarried sister of Peter's mother, Princess Anna Mikhailovna Shcherbatova, took care of the orphan and his elder brother Mikhail.

As a member of the Russian gentry Peter Chaadaev was brought up in a highly anomalous class in Russian society. Russian rulers had traditionally called upon the gentry for service to the state. But in the course of the eighteenth century the attempted vigorous absolutism of Peter the Great had given way to the emancipation of the gentry from compulsory state service in 1762 and corporate privileged status in 1785.

The French revolution caused Russian monarchs to rethink implications of any further "westernization" of Russian society. During his short reign Paul I tried to curb the privileges of the gentry and bring them under his power but was largely unsuccessful. Alexander I had to reverse the trend of his predecessor in order to seek the support of the gentry in his plans for Russia. But the same acts which had given new status to the gentry as the only comparatively independent class in Russian society had also, in effect, eliminated the justification for one of the socio-economic factors upon which that status rested, namely, the possession of serfs. No longer could serfdom be justified upon the need to compensate the gentry as a class for obligatory service to the state. Though many of the gentry were interested in preserving serfdom even under these circumstances, a group within the gentry desired a change in the old order, even if this meant their loss of status as members of that very gentry. Some, such as Alexander Radishchev, had been imbued with the ideals of the enlightenment; others, such as Chaadaev, became motivated by religious and reformist-conservative ideals. But all shared a common attachment to western European culture, though each understood it in a different way. All were outfitted with a western European education. Chaadaev's early upbringing influenced his early orientation in this direction.

While he was still a youth, western European tutors were brought in to instruct him and his brother. His uncle, Mikhail Shcherbatov, chose these teachers from the professors at Moscow University: Professor Christian von Schloezer (1774–1831), son of the eminent German historian August von Schloezer, and Gottlieb von Buhle (1763–1821), professor of philosophy at Moscow University. Peter showed an early, marked interest in his studies and began to collect a special library of his own. Local Moscow bookdealers came to know him well; at the age of fourteen he corresponded with Didot in Paris about rare books.[5] Around 1808 Peter Chaadaev entered the University of Moscow. His nephew-biographer, Mikhail Zhikharev, describes him at that age as already well-read, well-educated, and gifted with a unique way of expressing his thoughts.[6] Chaadaev spent three years at the university. In particular, Professor von Buhle exposed Chaadaev to the works and ideas of Kant, Fichte, and Schelling. Chaadaev also attended the lectures of another of his former tutors, Professor von Schloezer, and those of Professor Kachenovski; both of these scholars represented the school of Russian "historical scepticism." Chaadaev's university friends included the writer and satirist Alexander Griboedov, his cousin Ivan Shcherbatov, who was to be implicated in the Semenovsky uprising of 1820, and the future Decembrists Nikolai Turgenev, Nikita Muraviev, and Ivan Yakushkin.

As Napoleon threatened Russia in 1812 Chaadaev

4

left Moscow University to join the army as a cadet officer in the famous Semenovsky regiment. He fought in such battles as Borodino, Pirma, Lutzen, and Leipzig; in the battle of Kulm, Chaadaev won the Anna Order, Fourth Class, as well as the Iron Cross. On April 1, 1814, he rode into Paris among the triumphant Russian troops which came to invest that city. In that same year Chaadaev was accepted into a Masonic lodge and received the first two Masonic degrees.[7] After his arrival in Paris, he transferred from the Semenovsky to the Akhtyrski regiment and was put in the Guard unit.

Upon his return to Russia in 1816, Chaadaev was promoted to the rank of cornet in the Hussar Guard Regiment, stationed at Tsarskoe Selo, near St. Petersburg. There began his intimate friendship with Alexander Pushkin. Chaadaev's other friends at this time included many of his old colleagues from student days at Moscow University; Alexander Griboedov, Ivan Yakushkin, Nikolai Turgenev, and the Muraviev-Apostol brothers. In December, 1817, Chaadaev moved to St. Petersburg. There he became aide-de-camp to Prince I. V. Vasilchikov, commander of the Guard Corps. In that same year Chaadaev was promoted to the rank of captain. In St. Petersburg he moved in the upper circles of Russian society. Chaadaev also belonged to various Masonic lodges in St. Petersburg, but by 1818 he forsook this passing fancy, just as some of his friends did about that time. He had reached the eighth degree of the lodge "Amis Réunis" which was soon to be suppressed.[8]

In 1820 the revolt of the Semenovsky regiment occasioned a change in Chaadaev's career.[9] As one of the aides-de-camp to the Corps Commander, Chaadaev was sent to Troppau, in order to relay information to Tsar Alexander about the Semenovsky revolt. Soon after this Chaadaev retired from military service. His request to be released from duty was accepted only after the police, who kept close watch on all the "liberals," opened Chaadaev's mail and found some remarks which showed that Chaadaev treated the favors of the emperor and of Vasilchikov in rather cavalier fashion.[10] In March, 1821, Chaadaev left military service for good. Part of the next two quiet years was spent on his aunt's estate near Moscow and part in the city itself.

On July 6, 1823, Chaadaev left Russia for western Europe on a trip which was to last three years. He visited London, Brighton, Paris, Florence, Venice, Verona, Rome, Munich, and Karlsbad. Along the way Chaadaev visited local bookdealers in his efforts to build up his personal library. Upon his return he was detained at the Russian border. His name had been linked with the members of the Decembrist revolt of 1825. During the lengthy investigation of August, 1826, Chaadaev did not deny his acquaintance with the leading Decembrists, but he could not have taken any active part in the uprising, since he had been absent from Russia since 1823. The customs inspectors found numerous "forbidden" books among his luggage.[11] Only after a thorough examination was he allowed to proceed to Moscow.

Chaadaev retreated completely from society. Many of his old friends who had been members of the ill-fated Decembrist uprising were in exile or in prison. In this period of seclusion from 1827 to 1831 Chaadaev produced his most important work, the eight "Philosophical Letters." Near his aunt's estate outside Moscow resided one of his few friends at the time, a young noblewoman, Ekaterina Dmitrievna Panova, whom Chaadaev had met in 1827. She and Chaadaev had engaged in discussions about religion and philosophy. In 1828 Chaadaev left his aunt's estate and returned to Moscow. Madame Panova and her husband also went to Moscow about the same time, and the discussions between Madame Panova and Chaadaev continued. In an undated letter she asked for Chaadaev's advice about her religious problems. He began writing what was ostensibly a reply to her but in reality he devised the letter itself simply as a literary vehicle, the first in the series of "Philosophical Letters" designed to express his views on Russian history and culture.

Handwritten copies of some of these letters became known to select members of Russian society. As early as the beginning of 1830 some of the letters were read and discussed in the literary circles of Moscow.[12] At the Sverbeev salon Chaadaev himself read two of his "Philosophical Letters."[13] Meanwhile the news of the July Revolution of 1830 in Paris caused Chaadaev to modify several of his ideas on western European political trends.[14] In 1831 Chaadaev's doctor encouraged him to move about actively in society again. He joined the English Club, one of the most select clubs in Moscow.

Chaadaev sought Pushkin's help in finding a publisher for his "Philosophical Letters." Pushkin's letter of July 6, 1831, to Chaadaev indicates that Pushkin had opened up discussions with the French bookseller Bellizard about the matter.[15] But nothing came of this attempt. In 1832 Chaadaev attempted to have parts from two of his "Philosophical Letters" (Letters VI and VII) accepted for publication by the Moscow publishing house of A. Simon.[16] Near the end of 1833 he took up permanent residence in the large home of one of his acquaintances, the Levashovs, on the New Basmannaya street in Moscow. He was to reside there the rest of his life. Each Monday a literary circle gathered at his apartment. Around 1835 or 1836 Chaadaev tried again to have at least two of his "Philosophical Letters" published in the newly founded *Moskovski Nablyudatel*. There was also the possibility that "The First Philosophical Letter" would be published in that journal, as well. However, the editor wanted some changes made in the text: all references to Russia and "we" were to be deleted and in their place the words "certain people" should be written. Chaadaev refused to do this.[17] In 1836 he sent a manuscript to Paris in the hopes that it might be published by a French journal. But this also never materialized.

Chaadaev also gave copies of the "Philosophical Letters" to the famous university professor Nikolai Nadezhdin, editor of the journal *Telescope*. Apparently Chaadaev did not think that "The First Philosophical Letter" would be published; however, when the censor passed on it, Chaadaev considered this an act of Providence. Nadezhdin's magazine *Telescope* was headed for financial ruin. Nadezhdin felt that the publication of "The First Philosophical Letter" would create a literary sensation.[18] It did, as we have seen.[19] The furor about "The First Philosophical Letter" continued well into the 1830's. Popular discussion about it broke out, even in fairly public circles in Moscow.[20]

Like most of the Russians of his day, the poet Zhukovsky criticized Chaadaev's point of view.[21] But at least two Russian intellectuals recognized the "First Philosophical Letter" as an expression of true patriotism: Lermontov and Herzen. Lermontov felt that Chaadaev would be honored by posterity which would declare that "he loved his native land."[22] The most famous enthusiastic reception of the "First Philosophical Letter" came from Alexander Herzen while he was in Vyatka.[23]

No later than February, 1837, Chaadaev received some of his personal papers back from the government, and by October 30, 1837, the political and medical surveillance had ceased upon orders from the tsar.[24] But the seven other letters in the series of "Philosophical Letters" remained unpublished during Chaadaev's lifetime, as did his *Apologia of a Madman*. For the purposes of this study which concentrates on those two major works cited above, all subsequent events in Chaadaev's life are of relatively little importance.

Chaadaev had to content himself in the 1840's with the role of *salon* preacher-philosopher. During this period he became friendly with Alexander Herzen who had come back to live in Moscow from 1840 to 1847. He also continued his acquaintance with many of the leading Slavophiles and Westernizers. He heard Yuri Samarin defend his doctoral thesis in the halls of Moscow University. Samarin tried to justify Orthodoxy by a new Hegelian argumentation. Chaadaev objected to the attempt, though he admired Samarin's talents. Chaadaev also listened to Granovsky's lectures on the glories of the Middle Ages which he began to read at Moscow University in the academic year 1843–1844 and continued in 1844–1845. He heard Shevyrev's lectures on the literary glories of the Russian past in 1844–1845. The revolution of 1848 had a strong effect in Chaadaev's political philosophy.[25] When the Crimean War broke out in 1854 Chaadaev was able to see the ominous fulfillment of his Jeremaic prophecies; Russian cultural isolationism of Nicholas I had led to misunderstanding and war between Russians and western Europeans.

On the Saturday before Easter, April 14/26, 1856, Peter Chaadaev became ill in the afternoon. He was given Holy Communion and at four o'clock he had an attack of apoplexy from which he never recovered.[26] He received a Christian burial and was interred at Don Monastery, as he himself had requested.[27]

The most interesting epitaph on Chaadaev's life was written by one of his major opponents, the Slavophile Aleksei Khomyakov:

> Almost all of us knew Chaadaev, many loved him, and perhaps he was not as dear to anyone so much as to those who considered themselves to be his opponents. An educated mind, artistic feeling, noble heart—these were the characteristics which attracted everyone to him, and at that very time when thought apparently became immersed in a terrible and involuntary dream, he was especially dear to them, because he himself kept awake and awakened others —because in the thickening twilight of that period he did not let the lantern die out and played that game which is known by the name: "The Man's Himself Again!" There are epochs in which such a game is in itself a great service. Even dearer was he to his own friends by an undefinable sadness which accompanied the quickening of his lively mind . . . . How can one

explain his renown? He was not a public figure, but nevertheless, the name of Chaadaev was known by almost all educated people, both in Petersburg and in a large part of the Russian provinces, even though they did not even have any direct contact with him.[28]

An Analysis of Chaadaev's Major Ideas on History

TOO MANY WRITERS have tried to see more in Chaa-daev's work than was actually there.[1] Peter Chaadaev was simply a religious, social, and cultural utopian thinker. He had an *idée fixe*. It was the realization of the "kingdom of God" on earth, i.e., the eventual integration of philosophy and religion and then of all mankind into one universal Christian social and cultural system. His "kingdom of God" was not in the next world but in this one. It did not lie beyond but *in* history. But though Chaadaev was a utopian, he was no mystic.[2] He continually emphasized the importance of establishing proper material conditions in society, in order for men to progress towards this goal. A Romantic fascination with western European culture, particularly that of the Middle Ages, led him to an admiration of what he thought to be the historical influence of the Roman Church upon Christian culture. However, he was in no sense wholly satisfied with any of the Christian churches. His "social system" or "church," as he called it, was to be one of the future, a truly universal organization capable of uniting all mankind. From these convictions flowed all his interpretations of the mean-

13

ing of history, in general, and of Russian history, in particular.

History, to Chaadaev, is not the narration of the battles and reigns of kings, nor is it a chronicle of all that happened in the past. True history is the result of the meditations of philosopher-historians upon the religious and cultural implications behind the overt events of the past. The historian must not only describe, he must also evaluate. Chaadaev's own particular criterion for judging historical phenomena is based upon whether they aided or hindered realization of his ideal of unity. He believed in historical progress, but, like Guizot, Chaadaev modified the strict rationalist view of it. Instead of depending upon a "natural" ability of the individual's critical faculties, i.e., human reason, Chaadaev put his trust in the winnowing process of time. The endurance and recurrence of certain ideas in human history give men clues to the nature of human destiny itself. Men have always striven to achieve social unity and complete intellectual, cultural, and religious integration, hence this motif must be a basic drive in the historical development of mankind. In the past the most important persons were those who prepared men for the gradual acceptance of this ideal. In general, Chaadaev rated religious leaders and moralists above philosophers, since he considered that they had done more to raise the collective moral norms of humanity than most philosophers ever had. He favored such charismatic spiritual leaders as Moses, David, Epicurus, Christ, and Mohammed. By combatting the polytheism and multiplicity of moral codes in their day these reformers paved the way for the unification of mankind.

14

Concerning the study of Russian history Chaadaev simply contributed to a growing critical attitude towards the Russian past which was developing among some of the Russian intellectual circles of his day.[3] In his comparisons between the western European religiocultural complex and the Russian one he pointed up, first of all, the serious defects and weaknesses in the latter. In the midst of the nationalistic bombast of Official Nationalism under the aegis of Nicholas I Chaadaev's dissenting voice stood out.[4] He insisted that all Russian claims to greatness be compared with the cultural contributions of Western Europe. He found Russia wanting. He objected most strongly to all the super patriots who were trying to create a Russian superiority complex out of the dust of Russia's past. Russians, he felt, could never really be content with their past, simply because they have never even become conscious of the true meaning of it all.

Chaadaev presented the following arguments to prove that Russians were devoid of genuine historical consciousness: Russian history itself had no organic development. It had no intellectual or cultural continuity. The "history" of Russia was nothing but a series of illogical breaks with the past—from barbarism to foreign oppression to self-inflicted slavery. There were no conscious links among the past phases of Russian history. The reason for this lacuna was that Russians had never been motivated by a great, universal spiritual ideal. They acted only out of local motives of caprice or of violence. Whatever culture had come to Russia had been imposed from the outside. The advent of Byzantine Christianity in Russia brought with it a Christian culture in the Kievan

15

period but a narrowly confined one with a church which lacked the needed independence from civil authority. The Mongol Yoke which followed had cut off any contact with the flourishing Christian culture in the West. Despite attempts to gain contact with the West in the Muscovite period, Russia remained basically isolated and backward. While western Europe was moving ahead through the "glorious" cultural achievements of the High Middle Ages and Renaissance, Russia made no contributions of world import. While serfdom began to be abolished in the West, in Russia serfdom increased. Furthermore, while western Europeans took to the seas to spread their culture all the way to the New World and to the Far East, Russians remained landlocked and parochial and merely expanded geographically to the Oder and to the Bering Straits by means of force and sheer massivity.

It was Peter the Great who first attempted to make the Russians into an historically-minded people by linking them up with the mainstream of human history, namely, European history. Since Russia was a *tabula rasa,* Peter encountered no great conscious opposition to his reforms. The fact that Peter's reorientation of Russian society lasted after his death and continued apace proved, in Chaadaev's mind, that there could have been no survival of any supposedly "glorious" Russian past which could have formed the basis for sustained resistance to westernization.

However, though Chaadaev wanted further cultural relations between western Europe and Russia, he did not fail to see that Russia represented essentially a unique entity apart from western Europe. Long before Herzen or the Slavophiles, Chaadaev insisted on the idea that Russia was different from the West and that she could not simply take over Western institutions or way of life, since she did not enjoy the conditions out of which the Western institutions and way developed. Like Karamzin, Chaadaev distinguished between the West, i.e., western Europe, on the one hand, and the East. i.e., the Byzantine and Asian sphere, on the other, with Russia in between.[5] But though, in Chaadaev's mind, Russia was not a full member of the western European cultural complex, yet he felt that she was closer to the European rather than the Asian world.

Chaadaev does not fit into the category of Westernizer or Slavophile.[6] First of all, his major works predate the crystallization of the polemic between those two groups in the 1840's. Secondly, his peculiar admiration for the historical influence of the Roman Church was not shared by either Slavophiles or Westernizers. Thirdly, his interest in a new Christian universal sociocultural organization placed him outside these movements. Unlike most Westernizers, Chaadaev did not approve of the political and social trends in the Europe of his day. He did not look forward to a Russia imbued with the liberal ideas of constitutionalism and secularism, the hope of many Westernizers. In a lengthy polemical section of the *Apologia of a Madman* Chaadaev formulated part of the basic Slavophile position long before they themselves had formulated their stand. Chaadaev agreed with the Slavophile emphasis upon religion as the basis of all culture, but he disagreed with their estimate of Russian orthodoxy.[7] Furthermore, he took great exception to their evaluation of the role of Peter the Great in Russian history.[8]

It should be clear even to the cursory reader of

these documents that in the *Apologia of a Madman* Chaadaev did not retract the critical views which he had expressed in the "Philosophical Letters." In fact, the *Apologia of a Madman* was even more pessimistic about Russia's past than the "Philosophical Letters" had been. In the *Apologia of a Madman* Russia did have a "history," but only since the time of Peter the Great, i.e., only since the concerted assimilation of western European culture. But there was a shift in emphasis between the "Philosophical Letters" and the *Apologia of a Madman.* The lack of any conscious historical past in Russia which Chaadaev had envisioned as a definite weakness in the "Philosophical Letters" became a *possible* source of future greatness in the *Apologia of a Madman.* In Chaadaev's mind, it all depended upon whether Russians could be made to acknowledge the dearth of their past and in what way they would react to that awareness. If Russia's rulers would only follow the example of Peter the Great in continuing to assimilate the beneficial aspects from the western European religious and cultural heritage and to reject the adverse elements of it, then, unburdened by the contemporary nationalist petty jealousies of the West, Russia could emerge—but only under those conditions—as a new spiritual center for a rejuvenated Europe. A close cultural exchange among all the European nations and Russia could lead closer to the great apocalyptic synthesis, the kingdom of God on earth, the intellectual, moral, and cultural unification of mankind. This was Chaadaev's grand dream. But Chaadaev found no disciples in the Russians of his day to pursue it. Like most dreams, the significance of this one lay less in the possibilities of its realization than in the deep-seated motives which it uncovered. Chaadaev's motivation is clear. He definitely takes his place among those thinkers who reject the Russian tendency towards isolationism from Europe and advocate not a wall between Russia and Europe, but renewed contact within the common cultural context. Chaadaev was not just a Russian; he was a "good European."

The Philosophical Letters Addressed to a Lady

LETTER I

Adveniat regnum tuum

Madame,

It is your frankness and your sincerity that I love and respect most of all. So you can imagine what a surprise I was bound to get from your letter! These were the amiable traits of yours which charmed me from the moment I met you and which also induced me to talk with you about religion. Everything in your environment constrained me to remain silent. So imagine once again what a surprise was in store for me when I received your letter.[1] Madame, that is all I can say to you about the opinion which you presume that I have formed about your character. Let us drop the subject and proceed at once to the serious portion of your letter.

First, what is the source of this intellectual disturbance which perturbs and fatigues you so, you say, even to the point of impairing your health? Could this then be the unfortunate result of our talks? The emotion newly-awakened in your heart should have brought you calm and peace; instead it has caused you some anxiety, scruples, almost feelings of remorse. But should

23

I be surprised at that? It is the natural effect of that disastrous condition which encroaches upon all hearts and minds in our country. You merely yielded to the influence of forces which dominate everything here from the highest strata of society to the slave who exists only for the pleasure of his master.

Besides, how could you have rebuffed it? The traits which distinguish you from the crowd must also render you particularly susceptible to the bad effects of the air which you breathe. Could the little which I have allowed myself to say to you bring stability to your ideas amid all that surrounds you? Could I purify the atmosphere in which we live? I should have anticipated the result, and I did anticipate it. That is the reason for these frequent hesitations so little effective in bringing conviction into your soul and which must have naturally bewildered you. Besides, if I had not been convinced that, no matter what troubles it may cause in your heart, partially awakened religious sentiment is better than complete lethargy I would have been forced to regret my zeal. But these clouds which overcast your sky today will be dissolved one day, I hope, into redeeming dew which will impregnate the seed sown in your heart, and the effect which some insignificant words have produced upon you is my assurance of the greater effects which your own intellectual labor will certainly produce as a result. Madame, surrender yourself without fear to emotions which the religious ideas will summon within you; only pure feelings can issue from this pure source.

Now with reference to exterior circumstances, be

content for the time being with the knowledge that only the teaching founded upon the supreme principle of unity and of the direct transmission of truth in an uninterrupted succession of its ministers can be the one most in accord with the true spirit of religion; for it is epitomized in the idea of fusing all moral forces upon the earth into a simple thought, into a simple sentiment, and into the gradual establishment of a social system or church, which must make truth reign among men. Every other teaching, by the sole fact of its separation from the original doctrine, wholly rejects the effect of this sublime invocation of the Saviour: "My father, I beg you that they may be one as we are one,"[2] and does not want God's reign upon earth. But from this it does not follow that you are bound to profess this truth before the world; your vocation certainly does not lie in this. On the contrary, the very principle from which this truth is derived obliges you, in view of your position in society, to look upon this truth as an inner firebrand for your faith, and nothing more. I consider myself fortunate for having contributed to turning your ideas towards religion, but I would feel very wretched, Madame, if at the same time I may have caused your conscience perplexities which, in the long run, could only make your faith grow cold.

I believe I told you once that the best way of preserving religious sentiment is to conform to all the customs prescribed by the Church. This exercise in submission, which includes more than is commonly imagined, and which the greatest minds have imposed upon themselves after conscious reflection, is genuine worship rendered to God. Nothing strengthens the spirit in its faith as much as the rigorous practice of all the obligations which relate to the faith. Moreover, most of the rites in the Christian religion which emanate from supreme reason are a truly life-giving force for one who knows how to become permeated with the truths which they express. There is only one exception to this otherwise wholly general rule, namely, when within himself a man finds beliefs of an order superior to that which the masses profess, beliefs which elevate the soul to the very source of all our certitudes yet which do not contradict but, on the contrary, support the popular beliefs; then, and only then, is it permissible to neglect the exterior observances, in order to devote oneself better to more important works. But woe to him who mistakes the illusions of his conceit, the deceptions of his reason, for extraordinary illuminations releasing him from the general law! Madame, is there anything better for you to do than to clothe yourself in this robe of humility which becomes your sex so well? Believe me, this can best calm your disturbed spirits and infuse some sweetness into your existence.

Even from the standpoint of worldly ideas, for a woman whose cultivated mind is able to find charm in study and in the serious emotions of meditation, I ask you, is there a way of life more natural than quite an earnest one, devoted in large part to the thought and practice of religion? In your readings, you say, nothing appeals to your imagination as much as scenes from the lives of tranquil and serene persons; scenes which, like those of a beautiful countryside at close of day, calm the soul and remove us for a moment from a painful or insipid reality. Well, these are not fantastic paintings; it depends entirely upon you to make one of these charming fictions real; you have all the necessary requirements for it. You see that I do not preach a very austere morality. It is in your tastes, in the most pleasant dreams of your imagination that I am going to find that which can bring peace into your soul.

There is a certain aspect of life which bears no relationship to physical being but which refers to intellectual being; it must not be disregarded; there is a diet for the soul just as there is one for the body; one must learn how to submit oneself to it. That is an old adage, I realize, but I believe that very often it still has all the merits of an innovation in our country. One of the most deplorable things in our unique civilization is that we are still just beginning to discover truths which are trite elsewhere—even among people less advanced than we in certain respects. That follows from the fact that we have never advanced along with other people; we are not related to any of the great human families; we belong neither to the West nor to the East, and we possess the traditions of neither. Placed, as it were, outside of the times, we have not been affected by the universal education of mankind. This admirable linking of human ideas throughout the passing centuries, this history of the human spirit which led the human spirit to the position which it occupies in the rest of the world today, had no effect upon us. What has long since constituted the very basis of social life in other lands is still only theory and speculation for us. And, I really must say it to you, Madame, you who are so fortunately disposed to gather all that is good and true on earth and to neglect nothing which affords the sweetest and purest joys of the soul, what have you accomplished, I ask you, with all these advantages? You are still looking not for something to fill up your life, but merely your day. You lack the very things which form the necessary framework of life elsewhere, where all the daily events are ordered so naturally, a condition as indispensable for a wholesome, moral existence as fresh air is for healthy, physical existence. You realize that I am not yet referring either to moral principles or to philosophical maxims but simply to a well-ordered life, to those habits and those patterns of the intellect, which provide leisure for the mind and impose a regular movement upon the soul.

Look around you. Do we not all have one foot in the air? It looks as if we were all travelling. There is no definite sphere of existence for anyone, no good habits, no rule for anything at all; not even a home; nothing which attracts or awakens our endearment or affections, nothing lasting, nothing enduring; everything departs, everything flows away, leaving no traces either without or within ourselves. In our houses we are like campers; in our families we are like strangers; in our cities we are like nomads, more nomadic than the herdsmen who let their animals graze on our steppes, for they are more bound to their deserts than we to our cities. And do not think for a moment that this is something unimportant. Poor souls that we are! Let us not add ignorance of ourselves to our other miseries, and let us not aspire to the life of pure intellects; rather let us learn how to live sensibly within our given situation. But first let us talk some more about our country; we shall not go beyond our theme. Without this preamble you could not understand what I have to say to you.

For all peoples there is a time of violent agitation, passionate restlessness, and activity without conscious motivation. During that time men are physically and intellectually world-wanderers. This is the age of great passions, great emotions, great enterprises of the people. People are then vehemently aroused without any apparent object but not without benefit for their future descendants. Each society has undergone these periods. They furnish it with its most vivid recollections, its myths, its poetry, all its strongest and most fertile ideas. These are necessary bases of society. Otherwise societies would not have anything within their memory to which they would cling, anything towards which they could feel affection; they would merely cling to the dust of their soil. This interesting epoch in a people's history is the adolescence of the people. It is the moment in which their faculties develop most powerfully, and their memory of it constitutes the joy and the edification of their age of maturity. We, on the other hand, have nothing like that. First a brutal barbarism,[3] then crude superstition,[4] after that fierce, degrading foreign domination by strangers[5] whose spirit was later inherited by the national government[6]

—that is the sad history of our youth. Our history experienced nothing remotely similar to this age of exuberant activity, this exalted play of the moral powers of the people. The epoch of our social life which corresponds to this moment was filled by a dull and somber existence without vigor and without energy, in which the only thing that animated us was crime, the only thing that pacified us was slavery. No charming memories and no gracious images live in our memory, no forceful lessons in our national tradition. Glance over all the centuries through which we have lived, all the land which we cover, you will find not one endearing object of remembrance, not one venerable monument which might evoke powerfully bygone eras and might vividly and picturesquely depict them again for you. We live only in the most narrow kind of present without a past and without a future in the midst of a shallow calm. And if we stir sometimes, it is neither with hope nor desire for some common good, but with the puerile frivolity of the child who raises himself up and lifts his hands towards the rattle which the nurse shows to him.

Genuine human development in society cannot begin for any nation until life has become better organized, easier, sweeter than amid the incertitudes of this first epoch. As long as societies swing back and forth without convictions and without rules, even for routine matters, and as long as life is not organized, how can you expect the seeds of the good to take root? There persists the chaotic fermentation of things in the moral sphere, similar to the eruptions of the globe which preceded the present state of the planet. We are still at that stage.

Our early years, spent in immobile brutishness, have left no trace in our minds, and we do not have any individuality upon which to base our thoughts; but, isolated by a strange destiny from the universal movement of humanity, we have absorbed nothing, not even traditive ideas of mankind. It is upon these ideas, however, that the life of people is based; it is from these ideas that the future of people unfolds and from them comes their moral development. If we wish to take up a position similar to that of other civilized people, we must, in a certain sense, repeat the whole education of mankind. For this purpose we have the history of humanity and the results from the passing of the centuries before us. Undoubtedly this task is difficult, and it is not perhaps possible for a man to exhaust this vast subject, but, above all, it is necessary to realize the question involved: what is this education of the human race, what is the place which we occupy in the general order?

Peoples live only by the strong impressions which the past leaves upon their minds and by contact with other peoples. Thus, each individual senses his relationship to humanity as a whole. "What is the life of man worth," asks Cicero, "if the memory of past facts fails to succeed in integrating the present with the past?" But, as for us, who have come into the world like illegitimate children without a heritage, without a link with the men who preceded us on earth, we possess within our hearts no teachings prior to our own

31

existence. Each one of us must individually try to mend the rift broken within the family. What is habit and instinct in other people must be forced into our heads with hammer blows. Our memories do not go back beyond yesterday; we are, in a manner of speaking, strangers to our own selves. We move so peculiarly in time that, as we advance, each preceding moment escapes us irrevocably. This is a natural consequence of a culture based wholly upon importation and imitation. With us there is no inner development, no natural progression; new ideas sweep away the old, because they do not proceed from those old ones but come to us out of the blue. Since we only adopt ready-made ideas, the indelible characteristics which a movement of progressive ideas engraves upon men's minds and gives them power, does not even make an impression upon our intellects. We grow but we do not mature; we advance but in an oblique line, i.e., in a line which does not lead to any goal. We resemble children who have not been taught to think for themselves, and who, having become adults, have nothing of their own; all their knowledge lies on the surface of their existence, their whole soul exists outside themselves. That is our precise situation.

Peoples are moral beings just as individuals are. It takes centuries to educate them, just as it takes years to educate a person. In a sense, it can be said that we are an exceptional people. We are one of those nations which does not seem to form an integral part of humanity, but which exists only to provide some great lesson for the world. The lesson which we are destined to provide will assuredly not be lost, but who knows when we shall find ourselves amid humanity and how much misery we shall experience before the fulfillment of our destiny?

Europeans have a common physiognomy, a family resemblance. Despite the general division of these people into Latin and Teutonic branches, into the southern and the northern, there is a common bond which unites them in one whole, evident to anyone who has profoundly studied their history. You know that not very long ago all of Europe was called Christendom and this word had its place in public law. Besides this general characteristic, each of these people has a particular characteristic, but all that is simply part of the history and tradition of each and forms the hereditary patrimony of ideas among these people. In Europe each individual enjoys his share of the heritage; without strain or work during his lifetime each collects and utilizes notions disseminated in society. Draw the comparison yourself and see what elementary ideas we can acquire in this way during our daily lives, in order to use them, for better or worse, in molding our lives. And note that this is not a question of study or reading, nor has it anything to do with literature or science; it is simply the contact of intellects; in the crib the child is seized by these ideas which surround him amid his games, and are communicated to him by his mother's caresses; finally, under the form of diverse emotions these ideas permeate the marrow of his bones along with the air which he breathes and have formed his moral being even before he is sent out into the world and society. So you want to know what these ideas are? They are the ideas of duty, justice, law, and order. They originate in the very events which have built up society; they are the integral elements in the social world of these countries. This is the atmosphere of the West; it is more than history, more than psychology; it is the physiology of the European. What have you to substitute for that in our country?

I do not know whether or not we can deduce something perfectly absolute from what I have just said and from this derive some rigorous principle, but it is obvious that, when a nation's thoughts cannot be connected with any set of ideas gradually and progressively developed in society, and when its participation in the general movement of the human spirit was confined to a blind, superficial, often awkward imitation of other nations, then this strange situation must powerfully influence the spirit of each individual in that nation. As a result, you will find that we all lack a certain self-confidence, method of thought, and logic. We are unfamiliar with the western syllogism. There is something close to frivolity in our best minds. The best ideas for lack of any relationship and consistency are paralyzed like sterile dazzlements in our heads. It is in man's nature to lose himself when he does not find the means of referring his condition to what preceded and what follows him; then all consistency, all certitude escapes him; without the feeling of continuity to guide him, he discovers that he has wandered aimlessly in the world. There are some of these lost souls in every land, but in ours it is a common characteristic.

It is not this lightness of spirit which the French were once accused of and which was, by the way, just an uncomplicated way of understanding reality, which excluded neither intellectual profundity nor breadth and endowed human affairs with an infinite amount of gracefulness and charm; it is really the carelessness of a life without experience and conjecture, one which is unrelated to anything more than the ephemeral existence of the individual detached from the species and which adheres neither to honor nor to the advancement of any community of ideas or interests whatever —not even to the family inheritances and to this fund of prescriptions and perspectives which regulate both public and private life in an order of things founded upon the recollection of the past and the probable outcome of the future. We have absolutely no universal ideas; everything is individual, volatile, and incomplete. Even in our glances I find that there is something strangely vague, cold, uncertain, resembling somewhat the features of people placed at the lowest rung of the social ladder. In foreign lands, especially in the south, where physiognomies are so lively and so expressive, I often compared the faces of the inhabitants to those of my compatriots and I was struck by the sullenness in ours.

Some foreigners have credited us with a kind of careless temerity which is especially noticeable among the lower classes in the nation; but, only able to observe certain isolated effects of the national character, they were not able to assess the whole. They did not realize that the same principle which makes us so bold sometimes also makes us always incapable of profundity and perseverance; they failed to see that what renders us so indifferent to the hazards of life also renders us equally indifferent to good and evil, to truth and falsehood, and that this very characteristic deprives us of all the incentives which urge men along the paths of improvement; they did not perceive that it is precisely this slothful audacity which explains the fact that in our country even the upper classes are not, sad to say, exempt from vices which belong only to the very lowest classes in other places; they have not noticed that, though we have some of the virtues of nations which are young and only slightly civilized, we do not have any virtues of nations which are mature and highly cultured. I am certainly not claiming that there are only vices among us and only virtues among Europeans, God forbid! But I do say that, in order to judge nations, the pervading spirit which constitutes their existence must be studied, for it is this spirit alone which can direct them towards a more perfect moral state and towards an unending development, and not such and such a trait of their character.

The masses are subjected to certain forces placed at the summits of society. They do not think for themselves; among them there is a certain number of thinkers who do the thinking for them, incite the nation's collective mind, and make it advance. While the minority meditates, the rest feel, and the general movement occurs. Aside from some stupid races which have become brutish and preserved only the appearance of human nature, this is true of all the nations on earth. The primitive Europeans, Celts, Scandinavians, Germans, had their Druids, their skalds, and their bards, who were powerful thinkers in their own right. Consider the North American people whom the material civilization of the United States is so intent upon destroying; among them there are men worthy of admiration because of their profundity. Now I ask you, where are our wise men, where are our thinkers? Who is there who has ever thought for us, who is there who thinks for us today?

However, situated between the two great divisions of the world, between the East and the West, supporting ourselves with one elbow on China and another on Germany, we ought to have united within us the two great principles of intelligent nature—imagination and reason—and incorporated the histories of the entire globe into our civilization. The role alloted to us by Providence was not that at all. Far from it, Providence does not seem to have been interested in our destiny at all. Suspending in our case its beneficent action upon men's spirit, Providence has left us completely on our own, has refused all involvement in any of our affairs, and has not cared to teach us anything. For us historical experience does not exist; ages and generations have flowed by fruitlessly for us. It would seem that in our case the general law of humanity has been revoked. Alone in the world, we have given nothing to the world, taken nothing from the world, bestowed not even a single idea upon the fund of human ideas, contributed nothing to the progress of the human spirit, and we have distorted all progressivity which

37

has come to us. Nothing from the first moment of our social existence has emanated from us for man's common good; not one useful idea has germinated in the sterile soil of our fatherland; we have launched no great truth; we have never bothered to conjecture anything ourselves, and we have adopted only deceiving appearances and useless luxury from all the things that others have thought out.

A peculiar thing! Even in the world of science, which includes everything, our history is not linked with anything and neither explains nor demonstrates a thing. If the barbarian hordes which convulsed the world had not passed through the country in which we live before precipitating themselves upon the West, we would scarcely have furnished a chapter in world history. In order to call attention to ourselves, we had to expand from the Bering Straits to the Oder. One time, a great man wanted to civilize us,[7] and in order to give us a foretaste of enlightenment, he threw us the cloak of civilization: we took up the cloak but did not so much as touch civilization. Another time, another great Prince,[8] associating us with his glorious mission, led us victoriously from one end of Europe to the other: upon our return from this triumphal march across the most civilized lands in the world, we brought only evil ideas and fatal errors which resulted in an immense calamity which threw us back a half a century.[9] We have something or other in our blood which alienates any real progress. Finally, we lived and do now live simply to serve as some great lesson to far-distant posterity which will become aware of it; today, in spite of what anyone says, we do not amount to a thing in the intellectual order. I cannot stop being dumbfounded by this void and this surprising solitude of our social existence. Certainly, an unfathomable destiny is partly responsible for this. But man is also responsible for it, as he is for everything which occurs within the moral world. Let us consult history again; it is history which explains people.

What were we doing as the edifice of modern civilization was arising out of the struggle between the northern people's energetic barbarism and the lofty religious thought?[10] Forced by a fatal destiny, we proceeded to seek the moral code which was to constitute our education[11] in miserable Byzantium, an object held in profound contempt by these peoples. A moment before, an ambitious spirit* had removed this Christian family from the universal fraternity: the idea we reaped was in this way disfigured by human passion. In Europe at that time the vivifying principle of unity animated everything. Everything emanated from it and everything converged in it. The entire intellectual movement of this epoch was directed solely towards the unity of human thought, and every impulse arose from this powerful need to arrive at a universal idea, which is the genius of modern times. Strangers to this marvelous principle, we became a prey for conquest.[13] And then when freed from the foreign yoke, had we not been separated from the common family, we might have profited from these ideas which had arisen dur-

* Photius[12]

ing this period among our western brothers, however, we fell into an even more obdurate slavery,[14] sanctified by the fact of our deliverance.

What clear illumination already burst forth[15] then in Europe out of the apparent darkness which had enclosed Europe! Most of the knowledge which the human spirit is proud of today had already been perceived and, in returning to pagan antiquity,[16] the Christian world rediscovered the forms of the beautiful which it still lacked. But we were isolated in our schism, and nothing that was happening in Europe reached us. We had nothing to do with the great work of the world. The eminent qualities with which religion had endowed modern people and which, from a healthy intellectual point of view, raises them as high above ancient people as those were raised above the Hottentots and Laplanders; the new forces with which religion had enriched human intelligence and the customs which submission to an unarmed authority[17] had rendered just as mild as they had formerly been brutal—all that passed us by. When Christianity was advancing majestically along the road which had been traced for it by its divine founder and was sweeping generations along with it, in spite of the fact that we called ourselves Christians, we did not budge. While the world was being completely rebuilt, nothing was being built in our land: we remained squatting in our hovels made of small joists and thatch. In a word, the new destinies of the human race were not accomplished in our land. Though we were Christians, the fruit of Christianity did not mature for us.

I ask you, is it not absurd to suppose as is generally done in our land that, without even bothering to find out how it was produced, we can in one stroke assimilate all this European progress, which occurred so slowly and under the direct, evident action of a unique moral power?

People understand nothing about Christianity, if they do not realize that in it there is a purely historical aspect which forms so essential a part of the dogma that in a certain way it includes all of Christian philosophy, since it reveals what Christianity has done for men and what it can do for them in the future. In this way the Christian religion is revealed not only as a moral system, conceived in the perishable forms of the human spirit, but as an eternal, divine power, acting universally in the intellectual world, and its visible action ought to present us with a perpetual lesson. That is the proper meaning of the dogma of faith in one universal Church as expressed in the creed.

In the Christian world everything must necessarily lead towards the establishment of a perfect order on earth and it does contribute to this really; otherwise Our Lord's word would be denied by the facts. He would not be with His Church to the end of time. The new order, God's reign which the redemption was to effect, would not differ from the old order, the reign of evil, which it was supposed to annihilate, and there would still be only this imaginary perfectibility of which philosophy dreams and which each page of history refutes: vain intellectual activity which satisfies only material needs and has always raised man to some heights only to precipitate him into a more profound abyss.

Come now, you will say, are we not Christians then and is European civilization the only way to become civilized? We are certainly Christians: but are not the Abyssinians, too? Certainly men can be civilized in a way other than the European one; is not Japan civilized even more than Russia, if we can accept the testimony of one of our compatriots? Do you believe that Abyssinian Christianity and Japanese civilization will produce this world order which I discussed before, and which is the ultimate destiny of mankind? Do you believe these absurd aberrations of divine and human truths will cause heaven to descend upon earth?

There are two very distinct things in Christianity: one is its action upon the individual, the other is its action upon universal intelligence. By nature they blend in supreme reason and lead necessarily to the same goal. But our limited point of view could not comprehend the continuity in which the eternal designs of divine wisdom are realized. We must distinguish between the divine action which is manifested at a given time during man's life and that which only takes place in infinity. On the day when the work of redemption will finally be completed, all hearts and all minds will become but one single emotion and one single thought, and all the walls separating people and faiths will crumble. But today each one should realize his particular place in the order of the general Christian vocation, i.e., what are the means which he finds in and around himself for participating in the goal proposed for the whole human society.

Thus within the society in which this goal ought to be reached there is necessarily a certain circle of ideas in which men's minds are moving, i.e., in which thought revealed from above is to mature and achieve its complete fulfillment. There this circle of ideas, this moral sphere, naturally produces a certain mode of existence and a point of view which, without being precisely the same for each person, yet with reference to us as with reference to all non-European people, forms a similar way of life, a result of this immense intellectual work of eighteen centuries, in which all the passions, all the interests, all the sufferings, all the conceptions, and all the efforts of reason have participated.

All the European nations went hand in hand, as they advanced together throughout the centuries. No matter what each of them may do today to go off in his own particular directions, they always find themselves on the same route. To understand the family development of these people, men need not study history: just read Tasso[19] and see them all prostrate at the foot of Jersualem's walls. Remember that during fifteen centuries they had only one single idiom with which to address God, only one single moral authority, only one single religious conviction. Imagine that each year on the same day at the same hour in the same words all of them simultaneously raised their voices to the Supreme Being during fifteen centuries, in order to celebrate His glory in the greatest of His good works: admirable symphony, a thousand times more sublime than all the harmonies of the physical world! But, since this sphere in which the Europeans live—the only one in which humanity can achieve its final destiny—is the result of the influence which religion exercised among them and, if up to now the weakness of our beliefs or the insufficiency of our dogma has placed us outside the universal movement in which the social idea of Christianity was developed and formulated, and if it has relegated us to the category of people who must profit only indirectly and very late from the complete effect of Christendom, then it is clear that impetus must be given to us, for it is Christianity which has produced everything over there. That is what I meant when I said that we have to begin the education of humanity all over again in our country.

The entire history of modern society occurs on the level of beliefs. That is the essence of genuine education. Instituted originally on this basis, education advanced only by means of thought. Interests have always followed ideas there and have never preceded them. So, beliefs have always produced interests and never have interests produced beliefs. All political revolutions were in principle simply moral revolutions. Man sought truth and found liberty and happiness. This approach explains the phenomenon of modern society and its civilization; it cannot be understood in any other way.

Religious persecutions, martyrdoms, propagation of Christianity, heresies, councils: such are the events which fill the first centuries.[20] The entire movement of this epoch, including the barbarian invasions, is linked with these efforts of the modern spirit in its infancy.

44

Formation of the hierarchy, centralization of spiritual power, continued propagation of religion in northern lands, that is what fills the second epoch.[21] Then comes the exaltation of religious sentiment[22] to its supreme degree and the consolidation of religious authority. The philosophical and literary development[23] of the intellect and the culture of moral life under the rule of religion completes this history which can be called sacred, just as much as that of the ancient chosen people. Finally, it is again a religious reaction,[24] a new impulse given to the human spirit by religion, which determined the present shape of society. Therefore, the great, or it can be said, the sole interest of modern people, has always centered upon beliefs. All the material, positive, and individual interests were absorbed in that alone.

I know that this prodigious striving of human nature towards its possible perfection has not been admired but, on the contrary, has been called fanaticism and superstition.[25] But, no matter what men may say, judge what profound imprint, for better or worse, a social development, wholly produced by one sole emotion, must have left upon the character of these people! Let any superficial philosophy[26] shout as much as it likes against the religious wars or against the stakes set on fire by intolerance; as for us, we can only envy the fate of people who, in the clash of convictions, in these bloody conflicts for the cause of truth, have created for themselves a world of ideas which we cannot even imagine—much less transport ourselves there body and soul, as we pretentiously claim we can.

Once more, assuredly all is not reason, virtue, religion in Europe, far from it. But everything is mysteriously dominated by the power which has reigned sovereignly there for a series of centuries; everything is the result of this long chain of events and ideas which has produced the present state of society there. And here is one proof among many: the nation whose features are most strongly delineated, whose institutions are the most permeated by the modern spirit, the English, has in reality only a religious history. Their last revolution,[27] to which they owe their liberty and prosperity, as well as the entire series of events since the reign of Henry VIII which caused this revolution, is simply a religious development. In this whole period real political interest appears only as a secondary factor; sometimes it disappears entirely or is sacrificed to that of religious conviction. And as I write these lines,* it is still religious interest which moves this favored land.[28] But, generally speaking, how could any European people, if it took the trouble to explore its national consciousness, fail to notice this particular element which, as a holy thought, was constantly the vivifying principle of its history, the soul of its social being?

The workings of Christianity are in no way limited to immediate and direct influence upon men's souls. The gigantic result which it is destined to produce ought to be simply the effect of a multitude of moral, intellectual, social relationships in which the perfect liberty of the human spirit must necessarily be given

* 1829

46

all possible leeway. So, it is understandable that all that has been done since the first day of our era—or rather since the moment when the Saviour of the world said to His disciples: "Go preach the Gospel to every creature"—together with all the attacks directed against Christianity fits in perfectly with this general idea of its influence. In order to recognize the accomplishment of his prophecies it is enough to note Christ's rule holding sway universally in all hearts, whether accepted consciously or unconsciously, voluntarily or involuntarily. Thus, despite all that is incomplete, vicious, evil, in European society as it stands today, yet it is nonetheless true that God's reign has been realized there in some way, because it contains the principle of indefinite progress and possesses germinally and elementarily all that is needed for God's reign to become established definitely upon earth one day.

Madame, before concluding these reflections on the influence of religion upon society, I am going to reiterate here what I once said about it in a work with which you may not be familiar.

It is certain, I said, that as long as men do not notice the influence of Christianity wherever human thought comes in contact with it in some way or other, even when it is only in order to combat it, they do not have a clear idea about Christianity at all. Wherever Christ's name is pronounced, this mention alone sweeps men along, no matter what they may do. Nothing demonstrates the divine origin of this religion better than this character of absolute universality, which allows it to infuse itself into men's souls by every possible means and makes it seize men's minds without their knowing it; even when they seem to resist it most it dominates and subjugates them by introducing into the intellect some truths which were not there before, by causing the heart to experience emotions it had never felt, by inspiring us with sentiments which place us, without our knowing it, in the general world-order. So, the function of each individual is determined by Christianity which makes everyone strive towards a single goal. If Christianity is considered from this point of view, each of Christ's prophecies takes on a palpable veracity. Then men clearly perceive the interaction of all the levers which Christ's omnipotent hand sets in motion, in order to lead man to his destiny without violating his freedom or paralyzing any of the powers which are truly his by nature, but, on the contrary, by adding to their intensity and infinitely exalting all their own proper potentialities. In this new economy no moral element remains inactive; the most energetic intellectual talents, as well as the warmest emotional capabilities, and the heroism of a strong soul as well as the abandonment of a submissive spirit, all have a place and an applicability. Accessible to every intelligent creature, associating itself with each pulsation of our heart, whatever it may be, the thought revealed from above carries everything along with it, and grows and strengthens itself even in the face of the obstacles which confront it. In a genius revelation is raised to a height unapproachable by the rest of mankind; in a timid spirit revelation moves ahead simply by hugging close to the earth and goes forward only step by step; in a meditative mind it is absolute and profound; in a soul dominated by the imagination it is ethereal and fertile in images; in the tender and loving heart it melts into charity and into love; revelation always advances in front of each submissive intellect by filling it with warmth, force, and clarity. See what a diversity of characters, what a multiplicity of powers, it sets in motion; what a variety of different qualities serve but one purpose; what a diversity of hearts beat for but one idea! But the influence of Christianity upon society in general is even more admirable. Roll out the entire picture of development in the new society and you shall see how Christianity transforms all human interests into its own interests, replaces material needs with moral ones everywhere, and in the domain of thought stirs up those great debates without parallel in the history of any other epoch or any other society—those terrible wars based upon religious convictions in which the people's whole life constituted a great idea and unlimited fervor; men will see everything become it and nothing but it, private and public life, family and fatherland, science and poetry, reason and imagination, memories and hopes, joys and sufferings. Within this great movement communicated to the world by God Himself, happy are those who have in their hearts the intimate realization of the effects which they produce; but all are not active instruments, all do not act with awareness; multitudes, inanimate atoms, inert masses, are necessarily moved blindly without recognizing the forces which set them in motion and without perceiving the goal towards which they are driven. But it is time to come back to you, Madame. I admit that I have trouble detaching myself from these general considerations. It is from the panorama presented my eyes from this height that I gain all my consolation; it is in the sweet belief of man's future happiness that I find refuge; when I am obsessed by the false reality which surrounds me, I feel the need of breathing a purer air and gazing upon a more serene sky. I do not believe, however, that I have wasted your time. It was necessary for you to know the proper way of envisaging the Christian world, and what we Russians have to do in this world. I have probably seemed bitter to you in speaking about our country; however, I have only spoken the truth, and not even the whole truth. Besides, Christian reason does not tolerate any kind of blindness, and least of all, that of national prejudice, since it is the one which divides man the most.

Here is quite a long letter then, Madame, and I believe that both of us must catch our breaths. At the outset I thought that I could tell you what I had to say in a few words. In thinking it over some more, I find that there is enough here for a book. Does it take care of things, Madame? Let me know. But, whatever your answer, you will not be able to avoid a second letter, for we have only begun to broach our subject. In the meantime, I would be very obliged to you if you would consider the prolixity of the first letter as a compensation for the time that I made you wait. I had taken up my pen on the very same day that I received your letter: then I became completely absorbed in some distressing and fatiguing preoccupations, and I had to get rid of them before putting myself in a frame of mind to talk with you about such serious matters; after that I had to recopy my scribbling which was absolutely indecipherable. This time you will not have to wait a long time: I shall take up my pen again no later than tomorrow.

Necropolis,[29] December 1, 1829.

If I succeeded in expressing my thought effectively
lately, then you must have come to realize that I am
far from thinking that it is only enlightenment which
we lack. There is not a profusion of it among us, it is
true, but we must resign ourselves for the moment to
getting along without those vast spiritual treasures,
accumulated through the centuries in other places; our
future lies somewhere else. Furthermore, granted that
we could have gained the knowledge we still need
through learning and contemplation, how could we
acquire strong traditions, broad experience, profound
awareness of the past, solid intellectual habits? All
these are the fruit of an enormous effort of all the faculties of man and that is what really forms the ethical
nature of European people and gives them an authentic superiority. Thus, our task now does not consist in
increasing the range of our ideas, but rather in correct-
ing those ideas which we possess and channeling them
in a new direction. As far as you are concerned, dear
Madame, this means that above all you need a sphere
of existence, in which the fresh thoughts introduced

into your mind by chance, and the new needs born out of these thoughts in your soul, could be effectively applied. You have to create a new world for yourself, since the one in which you live has become foreign to you.

Begin with the realization that the condition of our soul, no matter how sublimely it has been uplifted, is still necessarily dependent upon the circumstances around us. For this reason you must properly analyze what can be done in your social situation and in your own family, in order to harmonize your feelings with your way of life, your ideas with your domestic relations, your beliefs with the beliefs of those whom you see. Certainly much evil stems directly from the fact that our most profound thoughts stand sharply in opposition to the necessity of subordinating ourselves to social demands. You tell me that you do not have the adequate means to set yourself up comfortably in the capital. Well, so what; you have a charming manor-house: why not settle down there securely to the end of your days? This is a fortunate necessity, and it is up to you to make it as profitable as all the more interesting things which philosophy could teach you. Make your refuge as attractive as possible, fix it up with beautiful decorations, and why should you not put some selected finery in it? It is not a matter of sensual refinement; your efforts will not be aimed at vulgar amusement, but rather will make it possible for you to concentrate wholly upon your inner life. I beg you deeply not to neglect these material details. We live in a land so poor in ideal images that we can easily lose any sense of refinement, any understanding of the beautiful, if we do not surround ourselves with some pieces of poetry and good taste in our homes. One of the most astounding peculiarities of our unique civilization is its neglect of all the comforts and joys of life. We scarcely even think of sheltering ourselves from the extremes in the seasons—and this in a climate of which one may seriously question whether it was intended for the life of thinking creatures at all. If at a former time we imprudently settled down in this cruel climate, let us at least try to arrange things now in such a way as to be able to forget its harshness a little.

I remember that in the past you read Plato with great pleasure. Remember how carefully the most ideal, the most sublime of the sages from the ancient world surrounds the characters of his own philosophical dramas with all the good things of life.[1] Either they slowly walk along the charming shores of Ilissos or in the cypressed lanes of Gnosos, or they are sheltered by the cool shadow of an old plane tree, or they enjoy sweet moments of relaxation upon blooming grass, or else, letting the day's heat fall away, they take pleasure in the aromatic air and the calm, coolness of night in Attica, or else, garlanded with flowers and with goblets in hand, they lie in comfortable poses, around a well-decked table, and, only after having arranged them beautifully on earth, does the author raise them to the vast expanses beyond the moon, in which he liked to dwell so much. Even in the works of the strictest Fathers of the Church, in St. John Chrysostom, St.

Gregory of Nazianzus, and even in St. Basil, I could point out to you splendid descriptions of solitude, in which these great men found calm and lofty inspirations, which made them lights of the faith. These holy men did not think that they lowered their dignity in paying attention to such things, which make up an important part of life. In this indifference towards the good things of life, which some of us consider meritorious, there is something really cynical. One of the things which most retards progress in our land, I think, comes from the absence of any idea of art in our home-life.

Therefore, I would like you to set up a completely uniform and methodical way of life in this refuge, which you should decorate as beautifully as possible. We all lack a sense of order and research; let us correct this mistake. There is no point in repeating the proven gains and advantages of an ordered life; in any case, only a lasting subordination to specific rules can accustom us to submit effortlessly to the highest law of our nature. But a person must necessarily get rid of all that hinders an exact utilization of a definite order. One is often distracted from the circle of activity which one had in mind within the first hours of the day and the whole day is ruined. Nothing is more important than the first impressions which we experience, the first thoughts immediately after the deathlike state which separates one day from another.[2] These impressions and these thoughts generally determine the condition of our soul for the whole day. For example, the day can begin with a family quarrel and end with a mistake which cannot be corrected. Therefore, train yourself to make the first hours of the day as important and as solemn as possible; at once lift up your soul to all these heights within its reach, try to pass these hours in complete solitude, do away with all that can have too much of an effect upon you, or can diffuse your efforts too much; after such preparation you can painlessly meet those unpleasant impressions which catch up with you later and which under other circumstances could turn your life into an endless fight, without hope for victory. Add to this the fact that once a person has neglected this time of solitude and concentrated thought, he can never come back to it. Life engulfs you with all its pleasant as well as boring cares, and you will roll along in the unending wheel of life's incidentals. So, let us not allow the only hour of the day which we can have to ourselves to pass uselessly.

I admit, I place great emphasis upon the necessity of daily concentration and rectification in your soul; I am convinced that there is no other way of preventing yourself from being swallowed up by your surroundings; but you realize that this is still far from all. One idea, which permeates your whole life, must always stand before you, as a guiding light for every hour of the day. We come into the world with a confused instinct for moral good; in order to recognize it fully we need a more complete idea, which grows out of this instinct in the course of our entire life. To this inner travail you must bring everything; you must arrange the entire order of your life in relation to it.

But all this must flow from the silence of your heart, because the world does not sympathize with anything profound. It turns its eyes away from great convictions; a profound idea fatigues it. True fervor and concentrated thought must thus become part and parcel of your being, as they are not dependent upon opinions of different people but rather lead you with certainty towards a goal. Do not be jealous of society for its sensuous pleasures; in your own solitude you will find delights, which they cannot even understand. I do not doubt that, after you have accustomed yourself to the serene atmosphere of such an existence, you will begin to observe quietly from your cloister how the world flusters and how it disappears away from you; you will delightfully taste peace of soul. Meanwhile you should assimilate the tastes, habits, and attachments of your new way of life. You must free yourself from all vain curiosities, which foolishly waste and disfigure life, and first of all you must root out the stubborn inclination of the heart which is captivated by novelties, pursues daily gossip, and as a result, always greedily awaits what will happen tomorrow. Otherwise, you will find neither peace, nor happiness, but only continuous disappointment and repugnance. Do you want the stream of the world to be broken upon the threshold of your dwelling in this world? If so, then drive away from your soul all these perturbing passions, which are called forth by worldly events, all these nervous emotions brought about by the news of the day. Close your door against all noise and all the outbursts of the world. Avoid even all light literature, if you have enough determination; really it is nothing but that same noise, but in written form. In my opinion, there is nothing more incompatible with a well-ordered intellectual exercise than the thirst to read something new. Everywhere we meet people who have become incapable of serious thought or deep feeling, because they nourish themselves on these productions of the day, where one grabs everything without deepening anything, they promise everything without fulfilling anything, and everything takes on a doubtful or false tinge and leaves emptiness and indefiniteness behind it. If you are looking for satisfaction in the way of life which you chose, then you must never treasure any form of novelty.

There is no doubt that the more you bring your own tastes and inclinations into harmony with this way of life, the better you will feel. The more you reconcile the exterior with the interior, the visible with the invisible, the more easily you will travel the road before you. However, you should not close your eyes to the difficulties which await you. There are so many of them in our land, that they all cannot even be counted. Here we are not referring to any well-beaten path; it is a path on which a person has to fight his way through thorns and prickle, and now and then even across thickets. In the old civilizations of Europe definite ways of life have existed for a long time, so that there, when a man decides to change his environment, he simply has to choose that new framework into which he wants to move—the place has been prepared beforehand. The roles have already been handed out.

As soon as you have chosen a suitable way of life, then the people and objects arrange themselves around you. You have only to utilize them in the proper manner. It is a completely different thing in our case. How much annoyance and trouble it costs before you adapt yourself to a new environment! So much time is lost, so much strength is expended on arrangements, in order that those around you can learn to regard you in accordance with your new situation, in order to make a fool keep quiet, in order to quell curiosity. Do people here know what the power of thought is? Have men in our land experienced how a lasting conviction resulting from those or other causes permeates the soul contrary to the ordinary run of things by sudden intuition or by a direction from above; how it takes hold of the soul thoroughly, overturns our existence, and raises our being above itself and above our environment? What vivid realization has ever made a heart palpitate here? What man here has ever devoted himself to the veneration of truth? How then could a man who would like to devote himself ardently to his own beliefs, avoid clashing head-on with hindrances and objections from this crowd, which nothing has ever disturbed? You have to create everything, dear Madame, even the very air which you should breathe, and the ground under your feet. And this is literally so. *As for your atmosphere does it not consist of these slaves who serve you?*[23] *As for these furrows, which other slaves dug up by the sweat of their brows, is this not the very ground which supports you? And how many things, how much misery is contained in this one word: Slave!*

There is the magic circle, in which we all perish powerless to get out of it. There is the cursed reality against which we crush ourselves. That is why the noblest efforts, the most magnanimous impulses in our land come to nothing. *There is what paralyzes the will of everyone of us, that is what stains all our virtues.* Burdened down with a fatal sin, where is the soul, so beautiful that it would not choke under this unbearable burden? Where is the man who would be strong enough not to end up hating himself, living in eternal contradiction, always thinking one thing and doing another? Without even having noticed it there I am back once again at my first thesis:[4] let me linger awhile on this and then I shall return to you.

What causes this terrible ulcer which is destroying us? How does it happen that the most striking trait of Christian society is the very one which the Russian people renounced in the very bosom of Christianity? Why is the effect of this religion reversed in our land? *I do not know, but it seems to me that this alone should cause us to doubt the orthodoxy which we boast about.* You know that not one ancient philosopher attempted to conceive of a society without slaves, nor even to find anything to say against slavery. Aristotle, whom one may regard as representative of all the wisdom upon earth before the appearance of Christ, asserted that some men are born to be free and others to carry chains.[5] You also know that even the most stubborn skeptics admit that we are indebted to Christianity for the destruction of serfdom in Europe. Furthermore, you know that the first cases of emanci-

60

pation were religious acts completed before the altar and that in the majority of the emancipation texts we find this expression: *pro redemptione animae—* for the salvation of the soul. Finally, you know that the clergy set an example everywhere, by freeing their own serfs, and that Roman popes were the first to call for the destruction of slavery in the world subordinated to their spiritual authority. Then why did Christianity not have the same effects in our land? *Why, on the contrary, did the Russian people fall into slavery only after having become Christian, namely during the reign of Godunov and Shuisky?*[6] *Can the orthodox church explain this phenomenon?* Can it explain why it did not raise its motherly voice against the repulsive violence committed by one part of the nation against the other? And please, notice how abstruse we are despite all our exterior power and all our grandeur. During these very days the thunder of our cannons has again roared simultaneously at the Bosphorus and at the Euphrates.[7] However, history, which right at this same hour demonstrates that the abolition of slavery is one of the works of Christianity, does not even note that a Christian people of forty million souls remains in chains! The point is that the significance of any people among mankind is determined exclusively by their intellectual efficacy, and that the interest which they evoke is dependent upon their moral action in the world, and not upon the noise that they make. Now let us go back.

After what I have said to you about the way of life which I would like to see you adopt, perhaps you might have thought that I demand a life of monkish seclusion from you. But I am really referring to a sober, well-thought-out life, which has nothing to do with the gloomy harshness of ascetic morals. I am speaking about a way of life which can be distinguished from the life of the crowd only by a positive idea and by a fervor full of conviction, to which all other thoughts, all other sentiments would be related. This way of life may be combined with all the legitimate goods of life very easily: it even demands them, and human social relations are a necessary condition for it. Solitude has its own dangers, there are sometimes strange temptations in it. When centered upon itself reason feeds on self-made false images, and like Saint Anthony a person then populates his desert with phantoms, children of his own imagination, which pursue him into the world of men. Whereas, if you develop religious thought without passion, without violence, then even amid the noises of the world you preserve that inner attitude which renders all life's enticements and all its shocks powerless. You must find such a sweet and simple spiritual frame of mind, which would be able to join effortlessly the idea of truth and good with all the activities of the mind and with all the emotions of the heart. You must especially strive to comprehend the truths of revelation. The vast superiority of these truths lies in the fact that they are accessible to each thinking creature, that they adjust themselves to all forms of thought. All possible roads lead to these truths by the humble and blind faith which the masses profess without reflecting upon it, by profound knowledge, by laborious erudition, by the naive piety of the heart, by the reasoned inspiration of the mind, by the exalted poetry of the soul, but the simplest route is by means of recalling these frequent moments in life when we sense most deeply the action of religious fervor in our soul, when it seems that, deprived of all personal power, we are pushed towards the good despite ourselves by a superior force which elevates us from the earth and carries us to heaven. When, conscious of our own powerlessness, we open our minds very willingly to thoughts from heaven, it is then that the loftiest truths will flow, so to say, all by themselves into our heart.

When we frequently go back to the principle of our moral activity, to the moving force behind our thoughts and our actions, it is impossible not to see that a great part of what we do is determined by something which does not belong to us at all. It is precisely the best, the noblest, the most useful things occurring within us that we do not produce by ourselves. All the good which we do is simply the result of the ability which we have of submitting ourselves to the action of an unknown force: the sole, genuine principle of our own activity is the idea of our interest circumscribed within the limits of a given time-period which we call life. This principle is nothing but the instinct for self-preservation which we share with all living things, though we modify it to fit our particular nature. It is useless for us to attempt to be objective in our feelings and our actions, because it is always this more or less understood and more or less remote interest which directs us. No matter how much we ardently desire to act with a general good in sight, this abstract good, which we think up, is simply the one which we ourselves want. We are never able to abnegate ourselves completely; we always include ourselves in what we desire for others. Moreover, in the human expression of its law, supreme reason, yielding to our weak nature, has only ordered us to do unto others as we would have them do unto us; this is very different from the rest of philosophical ethics which claims to understand the absolute good, i.e., the universal good, as if it were up to us to form an idea of the useful in general by ourselves, when we do not even know what would be useful for ourselves. What is the absolute good? This is the unchanging law, by which everything strives towards its own end: there is all that we know about it. But if the idea of this good must guide us in life, do we not have to know something more about it? Undoubtedly, up to a certain point we act in accordance with the general law; otherwise we would possess the basis for our existence within ourselves, which is absurd; however, we act simply without even knowing why ourselves: moved by an invisible force, we can grasp its activity, study it in its effects, identify ourselves with it from time to time, but as for deriving a positive law of our moral nature from all this, that is impossible. A vague sentiment, a formless idea without authority—more we shall never achieve. All of human philosophy is contained in this terrible mockery by God in the Old Testament: See Adam become as one of us, having a knowledge of good and evil.[8] Now

I think you guess the necessity of revelation; and there is, in my opinion, what demonstrates this necessity. Man learns how to understand physical law, by observing the phenomena of nature, which follow in succession before his eyes according to a monolithic and unchangeable law. By gathering together the observations of preceding generations, he forms a system of knowledge, which is confirmed by his own experience, and the great method of calculation invests the system with the unchanging form of mathematical certitude. Although this order of knowledge takes in far from the whole system of nature and does not touch upon the universal principle of things, it nonetheless includes positive knowledge perfectly, because this information refers to beings, whose space and continuity can be perceived by the senses or else foreseen by definite analogies. In a word, here is the domain of experience, and insofar as experience can provide certitude for the ideas which it introduces into our mind, experience can make the physical world known to us. You are fully aware of the fact that this certitude can enable us to foresee certain phenomena a long time before they happen and even gives us the power of acting on inert matter with incredible force.

There, we have indicated the means of positive knowledge available to man. If, besides this, our reason has a power of spontaneity, a principle of internal activity, independent of the perception of the material world, then is reason always capable of exercising its powers only upon the materials supplied for it? In the moral order to what aim will man apply these means?

What must man observe in order to discover the law of the moral order? The nature of the intellect, is that not so? But is the nature of the intellect made just like material nature? Is it not free? Does it not follow the law which it imposes upon itself? Thus, if we study the intellect in its exterior and interior effects, what do we learn? That it is free, that is all. And if by chance in this study we once hit upon something absolute, would not our sense of freedom lure us back at that instant necessarily into the very same circle of ideas from which we thought we had just gotten out of before? Would we not, a moment later, suddenly find ourselves in the same place? This circle is inevitable. But that is not all. Let us assume that we really were elevated to some truths, which were proved so well that the intellect was obliged to admit them absolutely. Let us assume that we had really discovered some general laws, to which an intellectual being must necessarily submit itself. These rules, these truths, would refer only to one part of man's whole life, his earthly life; they would not have anything to do with the other part, which is fully unknown to us, whose mystery cannot be revealed by any kind of analogy. In what way, then, can these rules be the true laws of intellectual being, since they only refer to a part of our existence, one moment in our life? So that, even if we could discover these laws on the basis of experience, they could only be the laws for one period of time, experienced by our spiritual nature, and in this case how can we acknowledge them as laws of nature? Would this not be tantamount to holding that for each age-group

there is a special medical science, and so that in order
to cure, for example, a sick baby, it is useless to know
the infirmities of mature growth, that in order to prescribe a way of life suitable for youth, it is not necessary to know what is suitable for man in general, that
the state of our health is not determined by the state
of our health in all moments of our lives and, finally,
that we can let ourselves become addicted to all sorts
of aberrations and excesses in certain periods of our
lives without being punished the rest of our days? I
ask you, what would you think of a man who would
hold that there is one moral code for youth, another
for maturity, and still another for old age, and that
education is confined only to the child and the young
man? Well, this is exactly what all your ethics of the
philosophers assert. It teaches us what we must do
today, but it does not concern itself with what will
happen to us tomorrow. But what is future life if not
the tomorrow of our present life?

All this leads us to the following conclusion: the
entire life of an intelligent being embraces two worlds,
only one of which is known, and since every moment of
life is indissolubly linked with all subsequent moments,
which make up life, then it is evident that through our
own powers it is impossible for us to attain the recogni-
tion of a law which necessarily has to relate to this
world and to the other one. Therefore, this law must
inevitably be taught to us by an intellect for which one
single world, a unified order of things, exists.

However, do not imagine that the philosopher's
ethics has no value, from our point of view. We know

very well that it contains great and beautiful truths which have guided men for a long time and which even now speak powerfully to man's heart and soul. But we likewise know that these truths were not thought out by human reason but were infused from above at different epochs in the universal history of humanity. This is one of the primitive truths taught by natural reason and one which revelation simply consecrates by its own supreme authority. Praise to the wise men of earth, but glory to God alone! Man had never advanced except by the firebrand of divine light. This light has always lit up the steps of man, but he has not noticed the source of the clear rays of light falling upon his path. It enlightens, says the Evangelist, every man who comes into the world.[9] It was always in the world, but the world saw it not.

The practices introduced by Christianity into the human spirit cause us to see the revealed idea only in the two great revelations of the Old and the New Testament, and made us forget about the original revelation. Without a clear notion of this first communication of the spirit of God with the human spirit of man, it is impossible to understand anything about Christianity. The Christian who does not find the answer to the great problem of moral existence in his own doctrines naturally has to turn to the doctrines of the philosophers. Now the philosophers are only able to explain man by man: thus, they separate him from God and inspire in him the idea that he is self-sufficient. It is generally imagined that Christianity does not explain all that we need to know; it is believed that there are moral truths which philosophy alone is capable of teaching us: this is a great mistake. There is no human knowledge capable of replacing divine knowledge. For the Christian the whole movement of the human soul is nothing else but the tableau of God's continuous action in the world. The study of the results of this movement simply furnish him with proofs for the support of his faith. In the different philosophical systems, in all the strivings of man, the Christian sees a more or less fortunate development of the intellectual powers in the world in accordance with the different situations and different ages of society, but he discovers the mystery of man's end not in the trepidant and uncertain agitation of human reason, but in symbols and profound images, willed to mankind through teachings, whose origins disappear into the bosom of God. If he probes into the theories in which earthly thought was formulated step by step, it is only in order to find these more or less obliterated traces of the original teachings, given over to man by the Creator Himself on that day, on which He made him with His own hands; if he concentrates on the history of the human spirit, it is in order to find within it supernatural illuminations which have never ceased enlightening human reason without reason's knowledge, by penetrating all the fogs, all the shadows, with which human reason so loves to surround itself. Everywhere he notes these powerful and indelible ideas which came down from heaven to earth, without which humanity would have long ago become entangled in its own freedom. And finally, he knows that once again it is thanks to these very ideas that the human spirit could take in more nearly perfect truths which God condescended to communicate to him in a more recent epoch.

And therefore, far from attempting to master all the fictions contained in the human brain, he only tries to comprehend as well as possible the Lord's way in the universal life of humanity. He is attracted only to the heavenly tradition; the distortions made by men are of secondary interest for him. In this way he necessarily comes to understand that in the ocean of human opinion there is a certain rule by which men can discover the boat of salvation which invariably follows the star placed in the firmament to guide it; an ever brilliant star, which no cloud ever overcast; it is visible to every eye, in all regions, and it remains over our heads both day and night. And if it is once proved to him that the whole arrangement of the moral world is the result of a wondrous union between the original notions put into our soul by God himself, and the action of our reason upon these ideas, then it will likewise be clear to him that the preservation of these elements, their transmission from century to century, from generation to generation, must have been determined by some special laws and that there are naturally some visible signs, by which it is possible to recognize among all the holy places spread throughout the world, that of the holy ark which contains the sacred security of truth.

Madame, before the world was ripe for the reception of the new truths, which were destined to spread throughout the world one day, while the education of humanity was being completed through the development of all its own potentialities, from time to time a vague but profound sentiment allowed a chosen few to foresee the luminous sign of the star of truth passing through its orbit. Thus, Pythagoras, Socrates, Zoroaster, and especially Plato had inexpressible glimpses of it, and their minds were illuminated by an extraordinary reflection. Their eyes, turned towards the point, from which the new sun was destined to arise, caught a sort of glimpse of its dawning. But they could not rise to the knowledge of the genuine characteristics in absolute truth, because, since the time when man debased his nature, truth has appeared nowhere in all its brightness, and men could not recognize it through the fog which covered it. But, in the new world if man still does not completely recognize these characteristics, then this is only because of a voluntary blindness; if he departs from the good path, then this is nothing else but criminal abandonment to the dark principle which was left behind in his heart with the single purpose of making his acquiescence to the truth more worthy.

Madame, you perceive, of course, the aim of all this reasoning: the consequences flowing from it become apparent to the mind by themselves. Next we shall deal with these consequences. I am convinced that you will master them without any trouble. Besides, we will not let our thoughts be broken any more by the digressions which we encountered along the way this time, and we will be able to converse more systematically and methodically. Good day, Madame.

71

LETTER III

Absorpta est mors ad victoriam[1]

Meditations of a religious nature led us to philosophical reasoning, and philosophical reasoning has brought us back to the religious idea again. Now let us go back to the philosophical point of view: we have not exhausted it. When one wishes to consider the religious question in the light of pure reason, then the religious question simply complements the philosophical one. Moreover, no matter how strong faith may be, it is beneficial for the intellect to realize how to gain support from the powers found within it. There are souls whose faith must be fully capable of calling upon national proofs when necessary. I believe that you belong precisely to this category. You have had too much contact with school philosophy, your religion is too recent, your habits remain too removed from this inner life in which simple piety is nourished and is satisfied all by itself; therefore, you cannot allow yourself to be guided by feeling alone. Your heart cannot get along without reasoning. Our feelings certainly receive tremendous intuitions; our hearts have great powers; but our feelings are with us only as long as they affect us, and our emotions cannot last continually. On the contrary, the things which we have acquired by reasoning remain with us every hour of the day. An idea which is thought out never leaves us, no matter what our spiritual mood may be, whereas the idea which is only felt escapes us ceaselessly and changes instantaneously, depending upon whether our heart beats more or less rapidly. And then, we do not pick out the kind of heart which we want; the one which we find we keep as is, whereas we are always in the process of forming our reason.

You state that you are naturally inclined towards a religious life. I have often thought this over and do not believe it. You mistake a vague feeling, provoked by circumstances, a dreamy caprice of the imagination, for a necessity of your nature. No, not so, it is not with this troubled ardor that a person devotes himself to his vocation, when one discovers it in life; one accepts then his destiny with perfect security, with completely calm certainty. Of course, it is possible and even necessary to transform oneself; for a Christian the assurance of this possibility and the consciousness of this duty are articles of faith, the most important of his beliefs. Christianity revolves entirely upon the principle of the possible and necessary regeneration of our being, and all our efforts should be directed towards this. But meanwhile when we have not felt the effects of our old nature dissolving within us and a new man made by Christ appearing in us, we cannot ignore any means which might hasten the arrival of this fortunate revolution. Moreover, it cannot occur until we have done all that we can to produce it. Besides, as you know, we do not plan to explore the entire domain of philosophy here; our task is more modest: it is up to us to find out not what is to be found in philosophy, but rather what is not. I hope that this will not be beyond our capabilities. For a religious spirit it is the only way to understand and to utilize human knowledge, but he must also understand the nature of knowledge and, as far as possible, he should consider everything inside the limits of his beliefs.

Montaigne said: "Obedience is the proper function of a rational soul, which recognizes a celestial superior and benefactor."[2] You know that he is not considered to be a credulous intellectual: today then let this thought of the skeptic serve us as our text: sometimes it is good to enlist allies from the enemy camp; that substantially weakens the powers of the opposition.

First of all, there is no reason other than subordinated reason; that is perfectly true; but that is not all. *Look, does man spend his whole life doing anything but attempting to find something to which he can submit himself?* First within himself he finds a power, which he recognizes as being different from the power which determines the movement occurring outside himself; he senses life within; at the same time he experiences the feeling that this inner power is not unlimited; he senses his own insignificance; after that he notes that an exterior force has power over him and that he must subordinate himself to it; there is his whole life. From the moment he gains the use of reason these two notions—one of an inner, imperfect

power, and the other of an exterior and perfect power
—permeate man's consciousness by themselves. And,
although these two notions do not come down to us in
a clear and precise manner, such as those notions communicated by our senses or transmitted by communication with other people, even so, all our ideas of good,
duty, virtue, law, and likewise their opposites, come
to us simply from this recognized need of ours to subordinate ourselves to something which is independent
of our ephemeral nature, free from the emotions of our
changeable will and the impulses of our turbulent
desires. *Our whole activity is only the effect of a force
which compels us to place ourselves in the general
order of things, in the order of dependency.* Whether
we acquiesce to this power or whether we oppose it—
it does not matter, we are always under its sway.
Therefore, we should simply try to get the clearest
idea possible of its action upon us and, as soon as we
have discovered something about it, we should surrender ourselves to it with faith and confidence, for
this force which acts upon us without our knowledge
never errs; this is the force which causes the universe
to advance towards its destiny. Thus, what is the great
question of life? It is this: what must be done in order
to discover the activity of the sovereign power upon
our being?

This is the way we understand the principle of the
intellectual world and, you see, as such it corresponds
wholly to the principle of the physical world. But one
of these principles seems like an irresistible force, to
which all is inevitably subordinated, whereas the other

principle seems to be just a simple force which acts in union with our own power and is to some degree susceptible to change by our power. This is the logical approach imposed upon the world by our artificial reason. But this artificial reason, which we willfully substituted for the portion of universal reason bestowed upon us in the beginning, *this evil reason which so often distorts objects under observation, which makes us see them differently from what they really are does not, however, obscure the absolute order of things so as to deprive us of the ability to recognize the primacy of subordination over that of freedom* and the dependency of our self-made laws upon the general law of the world. Therefore, if we accept liberty as a given reality, such reasoning does not hinder us from recognizing dependency as the fundamental reality of the moral order, exactly as we do this in the physical order. Thus, all the powers of the mind, all its means of knowledge can only really come from its docility. *It is powerful only by virtue of its being subordinated.* Human reason simply has to know to what it must subordinate itself. As soon as this supreme rule of all intellectual and moral activity is set aside, then we immediately fall into erroneous reasoning or willfulness. The whole mission of true philosophy lies then only in demonstrating this rule first of all and then showing the origins of this light which should guide us in life.

Why, for example, does the intellect not rise to the level of mathematical calculation in any one of its own activities? What is mathematical calculation? An intellectual manipulation, mechanical work of reason, in which there is no place for the reasoning will. Where does this prodigious power of analysis in mathematics come from? The answer is that it is a use of reason in full subordination to a given rule. Why does observation in physics provide us with so much? Because it overcomes the natural inclination of the human spirit, because it subordinates the human spirit to a direction diametrically opposed to its habitual way of thought: because it places the human spirit before nature in the humble position appropriate to it.* In what way has natural science achieved its great certitude? By reducing reason to a completely passive, completely negative activity. Finally, what is the basis of the brilliant logic which gives this natural science such enormous power? The logic of natural science enchains reason, it brings reason under the universal yoke of obedience and makes it just as blind and submissive as nature itself, the object of its study. "The only road," says Bacon, "open to man for mastery over nature, is the same one which leads to the kingdom of heaven: one enters it only under the humble appearance of a child."**

Furthermore, what is logical analysis if not an act of violence which the spirit performs upon itself? Let your reason go on its own and it will act simply by synthesis. We are able to proceed along the analytical road only by exercising an extraordinary effort; we

---

* Why did the ancients not know how to observe? Because they were not Christians.

** Novum Organum[3]

always fall back into the natural means, synthesis. Moreover, it is by synthesis that the human spirit began, and it is synthesis which characterizes ancient science. But no matter how natural, how legitimate synthesis may be, and often even more legitimate than analysis, even so, it is certain that the most efficacious energies of thought belong to the process of subordination, namely to analysis. On the other hand, if we look closely we find that the greatest discoveries in the natural sciences were always pure completely spontaneous intuitions, i.e., they came only from a principle of synthesis. But note that, although intuition essentially belongs to human reason and although it is one of its most active instruments, nevertheless it is impossible for us to be conscious of it, as we are of our other faculties. The point is that we do not possess intuition purely and simply, as we do our other faculties; there is something in it coming from a superior intellect because intuition is destined only to reflect this other intellect in our own. And that is precisely why we owe our most brilliant discoveries to intuition.

Thus, it is clear that human reason does not achieve its most positive knowledge purely by its own inner power but must be perpetually set in motion from the outside. Consequently, the real principle of our intellectual power is in reality nothing more than a kind of *logical abnegation*, identical with moral abnegation and originating from the very same law.

Besides, nature is not only presented to us as matter for experience and knowledge, but also as a rule for our reasoning process. Each natural phenomenon is a

78

syllogism with its major, its minor, and its conclusion. Consequently, nature itself imposes upon the mind the method which the mind must follow in order to learn how to understand nature; therefore, our reason simply submits to a law which is presented in the very movement of things. In this case, when the ancients, the Stoics, for example, who had magnificent prophetic sense, spoke about imitating nature, about obeying it, about conforming to it—since they were still much closer to the origin of all things than we, and since they had not yet split up the world into pieces as we— they merely proclaimed the primitive principle of intelligent nature, namely, that no power, no rule comes to us from ourselves.

As for the principle which causes us to act and which is nothing else but the desire of our own good, where would humanity be if the idea of this good were only a fabrication of our reason? Would not each century and each people have its own peculiar idea about it? How could mankind in general have moved ahead in its unlimited progress, if in the heart of man there were not a universal notion of the good, common to all times and to all places and, consequently, not created by man? Where do our actions get their morality? Is it not from this imperative feeling, which compels us to submit to law and to esteem truth? But then law is law only because it is not issued by us; the truth is the truth only because we have not thought it up. Sometimes if we set up as a rule of conduct one which we should not have set up as such, it is only because we do not have enough power to detach our judgments

from the influence of our inclinations; in these cases
our inclinations dictate a law for us to follow, but that
is because we think that we recognize the general law
of the world in this law. There are, without a doubt,
some men who seem to conform naturally to all the
precepts of morality; many eminent characters whom
we admire in history are like that. But the feeling of
duty is developed in these privileged souls not through
thought, but through those hidden impulses which
direct men without their knowing it, through great
teachings to be found in life without seeking them.
These teachings exert more power than our individual
thought and make up the general thought of men: the
mind is struck either by an example, or by a fortuitous
concourse of circumstances, which gets hold of you
and lifts you up above your own self, or else by favor-
able arrangement of your life, which forces you to do
what you would never have done without that; living
lessons of the times, singularly bestowed upon certain
individuals according to a law unknown to us; and if
a popular psychology does not take these mysterious
springs of intellectual movement into account, then
there is a more profound psychology which considers
the heredity of human thought as the first element of
intelligent nature and finds a solution to most of its
problems in it. So, when the heroism of the virtuous
or the inspiration of the genius are not the thought of
the individual, they are always the thought of past
ages. Whether we have thought it over or not does not
matter; someone had already thought for us before we
came upon earth. The feeling of duty, and hence

submission is necessarily at the basis of each moral activity, no matter how spontaneous or how isolated it appears.

Now let us see what would happen if man could push his own submission to the point of complete forfeiture of his own freedom. From what has just been said it is clear that this would be the highest level of human perfection. Would not each movement of his soul be produced then by the same principle which produces every other movement on earth? Then instead of his present separation from nature would he not be fused with it? In place of the feeling of his own will which now sets him apart from the general order and makes him into an isolated being, would not the feeling of the universal will be found within him or, to put it another way, the intimate sensation, the profound consciousness of his real rapport with all creation? Instead of this individual, isolated idea, which permeates him at this moment, instead of this personality which isolates him from all around him and clouds up everything before his eyes and which is not at all the necessary condition of his particular nature, but solely the consequence of his violent alienation from universal nature, in surrendering the fatal present *ego,* would he not recover the idea and also the comprehensive personality, as well as the whole power of pure intelligence in its original link with the rest of things? And then would he not at last begin to feel himself living in this narrow and unfortunate life, which induces him to relate everything to himself and to look upon the world only through the prism of his

81

own artificial reason? Of course not; he would begin to feel himself living the life which God Himself gave man on the day when He made him from nothing. The full use of our faculties is designed to discover this original life anew. A great genius[4] once said that man had recollections about some better life: a great idea not vainly flung upon earth; but here is what he did not say and should have said, and here lies the meaning which neither this brilliant genius nor any other from that age of human thought was able to attain—this then, that it is up to us to rediscover that lost, beautiful existence without leaving this world.

Time and space[5] are the limits of human life such as it is now. But, first of all, who can prevent me from escaping from the oppressive embraces of time? Where does the idea of time come from? From the memory of past events. But what is remembrance? It is nothing but an act of the will: this is evident from the fact that we remember only what we want to remember; otherwise the whole succession of events which has taken place during the course of my life would be perpetually present in my memory, would perpetually crowd together in my head but, on the contrary, even in the very moments when I give full freedom to my thoughts, I receive only the recollections which coincide with the present state of my soul, with the sentiment which moves me, with the idea which I am studying. We form our own images of the past just as we form those of the future. What hinders me then from repressing the phantom of the past which lies inert behind me, just as I can, if I wish, destroy the shifting vision of the future hovering before me; what stops me from freeing myself from this intermediate moment called the present—a moment so short that it is already not that same instant, when I pronounce the word which expresses it. We create all time by ourselves, that is certain; God did not create time; he allowed man to make it. But in that case, where could time exist? Could not this fatal thought of time, which obsesses and oppresses me on all sides, disappear completely from my mind? Could not this imaginary reality of time, which so cruelly dominates and crushes me, be totally dissipated? No more limits to my existence, no more obstacles to the vision of infinity; my glance plunges into eternity; the earthly horizon has disappeared; the heavenly vault is no longer fixed to the earth at the end of the immense plain which stretches before my eyes; I see myself in this unlimited continuity, not divided into days or hours or fleeting moments, but one continuity forever, without movement and without change, in which all separate beings are lost in each other and, finally, in which everything eternal subsists. Each time that our intellect succeeds in throwing off the fetters which the intellect itself forged, it understands this kind of time, just as that time in which it now subsists. Why does our intellect ceaselessly burst out of the immediate succession of things, measured by the monotonous swings of the pendulum? Why does our spirit unceasingly leap into this other world in which the fatal striking of the clock is not to be heard? The reason is that infinity is the natural atmosphere for thought; infinity is the only true time, and the other time is simply one which we create ourselves; why I do not know. As for space, everyone knows that thought does not reside in space; thought logically accepts the conditions of the tangible world, but it does not inhabit this world. Consequently, no matter what reality has been assumed for space, this is merely a fact outside of thought, and it has nothing to do with the existence of the intellect itself; though it may be an invisible form, it is nothing but a form under which the exterior world appears to us. Thus, space would be even less able than time to comprise this new existence, about which the conversation here revolves.

Here is this superior life towards which man must strive, a life of perfection, certitude, clarity, and infinite knowledge, but most of all, a life of perfect submission; a life which man once possessed and which is promised to him once again. And do you know what kind of life this is? This is Heaven, and there should be no doubt about that. We can already enter it even now, there should be no doubt about that. It is nothing but the complete renovation of our nature within the given conditions, the last goal of intellectual striving, the final destiny of the spirit in the world; I do not know whether each of us will achieve the glorious goal at the end of it, but the fact is that the definitive point of our progress can only be a complete fusion of our nature with the nature of the whole world, for only in this way can our spirit ascend to the perfection of things which are expressed by the supreme intellect itself.*

But so long as we still have not reached the end of our pilgrimage, so long as this great fusion of our being with universal being is not completed, can we not at least fuse with the intellectual world? Is it not within our power to identify ourselves on any level with beings similar to ourselves? Are we not capable of applying their needs, their interests to ourselves and transferring their feelings to ourselves, so that we finally begin to live only for them and feel only through them? Assuredly. Sympathy, love, charity—no matter what name you call our surprising capability of fusing ourselves with what happens around us—it is certain that it is inherent in our nature. If we so choose, we can mingle with the moral world so well that, provided we know about it, we may experience everything that happens in nature as if it were happening to us; more than that, it is not even necessary that events in the world preoccupy us extraordinarily; just the general but profound idea of the affairs of men, just the intimate consciousness of our real link with humanity is enough to make our heart start to beat for the destinies of all mankind and to make each of our thoughts, each of

---

* Here two things should be noted: first, that we did not have the idea in mind that heaven is wholly contained in this life, but only that heaven begins already in this life, since death no longer exists since the day on which it was conquered by the Saviour; secondly, that here, naturally, there is no question of a material fusion in time and space, but only a fusion in idea and in principle.

our actions harmonize with the thoughts and actions of all men in one harmonious whole. If we cultivate this eminent virtue in our nature, by developing it more and more within our soul, we will reach those heights from which the rest of the route which we have to follow will be revealed entirely; and blessed are those mortals who, once having achieved this, will be able to maintain this high level without sinking down again to the low level from which they ascended! Until then our whole existence would only be a perpetual oscillation between life and death, a prolonged agony; from this moment on, the law of the moral world would no longer be an impenetrable mystery to us.

But do things happen in this way in the world? Just the opposite. This law of intelligent nature can only be revealed very late and very obscurely in life; you see, it is not necessary to figure it out, any more than it is to figure out the physical law. All we can do is keep our soul open for this knowledge when it comes under our intellectual scrutiny. The moral law appears much less evident than the physical law, in the ordinary course of events, in the daily preoccupation of our mind, in the habitual drowsiness of our soul. True, it rules over us sovereignly, it orders each of our actions, each fact in our reason; and leaving us the consciousness of our own activity, by means of a marvelous combination, through a perpetual miracle, the moral law imposes a dreadful responsibility on us for all that we do, for each beat of our heart, even for each fleeting thought which barely skims our brain; but despite that, the moral law is hidden from our understanding in profound shadows. What takes place, then? Not recognizing the real principle which uses man as its instrument, man unknowingly creates his own law, and this law which he prescribes for himself out of his own initiative is what he calls the *moral law,* or else wisdom, the sovereign good, or simply law, or something else again.* And then in his blindness man ascribes all the certainty, all the absoluteness, and all the immutability of the real law of his being to this fragile product of his own hands, a product which he can arbitrarily break and really does break every moment in the day, whereas he is evidently only able to understand the inevitable necessity of the hidden principle and nothing more by means of reason alone.

Besides, although the moral law, just like physical law, exists outside ourselves and is not dependent upon our knowledge of it, nonetheless there is an essential difference between these two laws. A countless number of men have lived and still live without the slightest notion about the material forces behind nature; God wanted man's reason to discover that little by little all by itself. But no matter how degraded the intelligent being may be, no matter how limited his abilities, he could never be totally deprived of some knowledge about the principle which causes him to act. Deliberation and judgment assume necessarily the notion of good and evil. Take this notion away from man and he will not deliberate, he will not judge, he

* See the ancients.

will no longer be a rational being. God could not let us live one sole instant without this notion; He created us with it. And, placed in our soul in an incomprehensible way, this imperfect idea forms the entire essence of intellectual man. You have just seen what conclusions could be drawn from this idea, if men could succeed in restoring the idea to its original purity, such as it was given to us in the beginning; but men must also see what can be done by seeking the principle of all our knowledge solely in our own nature.

Sokolniki, June 1

LETTER IV

*"The will is nothing but a mode
of thinking. Whether the will is
conceived of as limited or unlimited, all the same some cause
which compels it to act must be
recognized: therefore it should
be considered not as a free
principle, but as a conditioned
principle."*

Spinoza. *De Anima*[1]

We have seen that each natural phenomenon can be
considered as a syllogism, but it can likewise be considered as a number. Men impose numbers upon
nature and consider it in action—this is observation;
or they reckon by means of abstraction—this is calculation; or lastly the quantities discovered in nature are
considered to be entities, and calculations are produced with them; in this case calculation is applied to
observation and science is completed. Here then is the
whole circle of positive knowledge. One must only
realize that, properly speaking, quantities do not exist
in nature; if they did, then analytical deduction would
be equivalent to a fiat of the Creator, because its perfect certitude would not lack a thing and would consequently be omnipotent.* Impotence then is error;
there is nothing higher than perfect truth. Real values,
i.e., absolute unities, exist only in our mind; in the universe only numerical appearances exist. These appear-

* In this case it would no longer be faith but algebra which
would move mountains.

ances which provide the basis for our apprehension of materiality are what give us the ideas of numbers: here is the foundation of mathematical conception. Thus, the numerical expression of things is nothing but an ideological mechanism which we construct from these data furnished by nature. First, we transfer these data to the field of abstraction, then we accept them as values, and after that we do what we want with them. Consequently, mathematical certitude also has its own limit; let us be on guard against losing sight of this fact.

In its application to natural phenomena certainly numerical science is fully sufficient for empirical reasoning, as well as man's material needs, but it is in the abstract order that numerical science is far from being sufficient in the same way for the certitude demanded by the mind. A fixed, unchanging, geometrical reasoning, such as most of the geometricians conceive it, is something as foolish as it is impious. If there were complete certitude in mathematics, a number would be something real. Thus, the Pythagoreans,[2] the Cabalists,[3] and similar men understood numbers in this fashion, since they ascribed all sorts of powers to numbers and found the principle and essence of all things in them. They were perfectly logical: they thought of nature as composed of numerical values, and they scarcely concerned themselves with anything else. But we who see something other than numbers in nature, we who seriously believe in God, are absurd when we dare to arm the hand of the Creator with a compass. We forget that measure and limit are the same thing, that infinity is the first attribute of divinity, that which forms, so to say, all its divinity; so that if we make the Supreme Being into a geometrician, we deprive Him of His eternal nature and bring Him down to our level. But pagan ideas still dominate us without our knowing it; that is what makes us fall into these sorts of errors. It is not true that number exists in divine thought; creations flow from God like the waters of a torrent, without measure and without end. But man needs a point of contact between his limited intelligence and God's infinite intelligence, which are separated by immensity, and that is why he loves to imprison divine power in the dimensions of his own nature. Here is also a real anthropomorphism, a thousand times worse than the anthropomorphism of these simple people who reduce the divinity to a being similar to them- selves, as they strive to draw near to God, because they are unable to imagine a moral individual made differ- ently from the one of which they are aware. In reality the philosophers do not do any better. "They ascribe to God," said a great thinker, who knew what he was talking about,* "a reason, similar to the one which they themselves possess. Why? Because they know of noth- ing more perfect in their own nature than their reason. But as divine reason is the cause of everything, and as man's reason is only an effect, what then can there be in common between these two reasons?" He says, "The most that the constellation of the Dog, shining in the heavens, and the dog, which runs about in the street have in common is, the name alone."⁴

* Spinoza.

You see, all the positiveness of the sciences which we call exact comes from the fact that the objects which they study are *quantities;* i.e., limited things. It is natural that the mind, since it can comprehend these objects fully, achieves in understanding them its greatest certitude. But you also see that, in spite of our direct participation in the formation of these truths, we do not, however, extract them from ourselves. The first ideas which suggest them to us are given us from the outside. Thus, the logical result issuing at once from the very nature of this knowledge which is the closest to certainty that we can get, is that this knowledge refers only to something limited, that it does not originate immediately in our brain, that we exercise our faculties in this order of ideas only upon the finite, and that we do not create anything. So then what do we find, if we try to apply the method offered to us by this knowledge to our other knowledge? That the absolute form of the known object, no matter what the latter might be, should be necessarily the form of something finite; that its place in the intellectual sphere must be located outside ourselves. These are the natural conditions of certitude. But on this basis where are we in relation to intellectual things? First of all, where are the limits of the data belonging to psychology and ethics? There are no limits. Secondly, where does moral activity occur? Within ourselves. Thus, can the method which the mind follows in the field of positive ideas be utilized in this other field? Impossible. And, in that case, how can we gain evidence? As for myself, I do not know. It is strange then that, as simple as this reasoning is, philosophy has never made it. Never has philosophy decided to clarify this essential difference between two spheres of human knowledge; philosophy always confused the finite with the infinite, the visible with the invisible, what can be perceived by the senses with what cannot. Even if philosophy sometimes changed its language, in the depths of its own thought it never ·doubted for one instant that it would be possible to understand the moral world in the same way as the physical world, by studying the moral world with instrument in hand, by calculating, by measuring intellectual dimensions, just like material ones, by experimenting upon intelligent being as upon inanimate being. Amazing, how lazy the human mind is! In order to avoid the effort, which clear comprehension of the superior world demands, the human mind distorts this world, distorts its own self, and then goes off its own way, as if nothing had happened. We shall see why the human mind acts in this way. Also, men must not think that everything in the natural sciences consists merely of observation and experimentation. One of the secrets of their beautiful methods lies in the fact that they submit to observation only what can really be an object of observation. This is a negative principle, if you want, but it is stronger, more fruitful than the positive principle itself. The new chemistry owes its progress to this principle; in general physics it is this principle which is at the basis of this abhorrence of metaphysics which became its principal rule and the foundation of its method since the time of Newton. But what does this mean? Nothing more than the fact that all the perfection of these sciences, all their might flows from their ability to restrict themselves wholly to their legitimate circle, that is all. But, what is the procedure for observation really? What do we do when we observe the movement of the stars in the heavens or the movements of living forces in the organic being, when we study the powers which move bodies or move the integral molecules which make up bodies, when we study chemistry, astronomy, physics, physiology? We conclude from what was to what is going to be; we link up the facts which follow one another directly in nature, and from this we deduce the nearest result. That is the necessary orbit of the experimental method. However, in the moral order do you know anything which happens by virtue of a constant, irrevocable law which would enable you to draw conclusions in the same way from one fact to another and thus foretell with certainty something about to happen on the basis of what went on before? It is not like that at all. On the contrary, here all is done only by virtue of divergent acts of free wills which do not recognize any rule except their whim; here all is the effect of the will and of the liberty in man. Then of what use would the experimental method be here? No use at all.

This is the lesson, provided for us by the natural course of the human mind in the sphere of knowledge in which it is given the possibility of attaining its highest certitude. Let us move on to the lesson contained in this knowledge itself.

Men have, of course, always cultivated the natural sciences, but you know that it has only been about a century since they suddenly rose to their present position of importance. Three things gave them the impetus which carried them up so quickly to this height: *analysis*—created by Descartes; *observation*—by Bacon; and celestial geometry—by Newton. Analysis, restricted entirely to the mathematical order, does not concern us here; we simply note only that it caused the application of an element of false rigorousness to the ethical sciences, and it prodigiously hindered their progress. The new way of studying the natural sciences, conceived by Bacon, is of the greatest importance for all philosophy, for this method gave philosophy this empirical tendency which determined the whole character of modern thought for such a long time. But, in our present investigation we are especially interested in the law by which all bodies gravitate towards one common center; we are going to study this law then.

At first, it appears that universal gravity takes in all the forces of nature; however, it is not the unique force in nature, and precisely because of that fact the law which gravity obeys is so profound from our point of view. Attraction all by itself not only fails to explain the world but does not explain anything at all. By itself attraction would simply turn all materiality into one formless, inert mass. Every movement in nature is produced by two forces which pull the movable object in two different directions, and this principle appears most clearly, especially in cosmic movement. But once the astronomers recognized that heavenly bodies are subject to the law of gravity and that the effects of this law can be calculated with accuracy, the whole

world-system became a geometrical problem, and with
the aid of a kind of mathematical fiction men now
assume the most general law of nature to be simply
Attraction or Universal Gravity. This force, without
which gravity would be worthless, is the *Initial Impulse* or *Thrust*. The whole teaching of the *Parallelism*
in the two worlds rests upon the precise idea of the
simultaneous activity of these two forces, as provided
by science: now we need only apply this idea to the
combination of these two forces, which we set up
earlier in the intellectual order, the one force which we
are aware of—our *free choice,* our will, the other,
which dominates us without our knowing it, the action
of an *exterior force* upon our being, and then see what
the consequences will be.*

The force of attraction is known to us through an

* The applications of the law discovered by Newton are
undoubtedly immense in the order of tangible things, and they
will become more numerous day by day. However, it should
not be forgotten that the law of the gravitational fall was
discovered by Galileo, the law of planetary movement by
Kepler. So Newton simply got the fortunate inspiration to link
up these laws. Moreover, everything related to this famous
discovery is important. For example, one illustrious geometrician complained that we ignored some of the formulae which
Newton utilized in his work. The point is well taken; no doubt
science would gain infinitely from the rediscovery of these
talismans of the genius. But is it possible to believe seriously
that the entire secret of Newton's genius, all his powers, are
evidenced in his mathematical methods alone? Do we not
know that this lofty mind contained something besides the
capacity for calculation? I ask you, would a thought of such
proportions ever have come to an impious mind? Would a
truth of such vast greatness even have been given to the

infinity of its effects; it is perpetually happening before our eyes, we measure it, we have a thoroughly certain knowledge about it. All this, as you see, corresponds marvelously to the idea which we have of our own power. Concerning thrust the only thing that we know is divine action upon our soul. However, we are similarly completely convinced of the existence of both forces. Thus, in both cases there is precise and exact knowledge of one thing, a vague and obscure knowledge of the other, but *complete certitude* for both. This is the direct application of this method of representing the material order of the world, and you see that it is presented to the mind in a completely natural fashion. But attention must still be paid to the fact that astronomical analysis extends the law of our solar system to all star-systems which fill up spaces in the heavens, that molecular theory accepts the law as the cause

world by a skeptical soul? And when Newton flew from the epidemic raging in London, in order to find refuge in Cambridge[5] where the law of materiality came to illuminate his mind and the veil of nature was torn down before him, how is it possible to imagine that there were only numerals in his godfearing soul? It is a strange thing that there are still people in the world who cannot suppress a smile of pity when they think of Newton writing a commentary on the Apocalypse. They do not perceive that the great discoveries, which the whole human race takes pride in, could have been made only by the real Newton, the genius, just as submissive as he was comprehensive, just as humble as he was powerful, and never the haughty man whom they want him to be. I repeat once more: where, then, has anyone seen an intellectual—I shall not even term him atheistic, but even one just indifferent to religion—extend the frontiers of science as he did beyond the limits which seemed to be prescribed for it?

behind the very formation of bodies, and that we have a complete right to consider the law of our system to be a universal condition of all creation, or close to it; in that case this point of view takes on an extremely important meaning.

Moreover, as for all the lines which we draw between different beings, all the imaginary distinctions which we establish for convenience' sake and in accordance with our own desires, does all that have absolutely anything to do with the creative principle itself? No matter what we do, do we not have an inner feeling about a reality superior to the apparent reality around us? And is this other reality not the only truly real, *objective* reality which includes all being and fuses us too with the general unity? In this unity then all differences fade away, all limitations which confront the mind because of its own imperfection and the limits of its own nature; and thus there is only one unique and universal fact left in all the infinity of things. Really the intimate feeling about our own nature, as well as our view of the universe, could not allow us to comprehend created being in any way other than in a state of continual motion. This is a universal fact. For this reason the idea of motion naturally has to precede every other idea in philosophy. But this idea of motion has to be sought for in geometry, because it is only there that we find it cleansed of all arbitrary metaphysics, and it is only in linear motion that we can acquire the absolute notion of any and all motion. And what does this mean? The geometrician cannot imagine any motion except imparted motion.

He is thus forced to start from the assumption that one thing by itself is inert and that every motion is the effect of an impulse imparted from the outside. Thus, in the loftiest abstraction, just as in nature, we constantly have to return to an exterior and primary action independent of the object under observation. The very idea of motion is thus logically inseparable from the idea of an action distinct from every power and every cause which exists in the very object in which motion operates.

And that is also why it is so hard for the human spirit to free itself from this old error which holds that all ideas come to the mind through the senses. It is quite simple: we would be more inclined to be doubtful about our own power than about anything else on earth, so the positive absurdity of the empiricist lies solely in the fact that this system attributes the material with an immediate action upon the immaterial and thus makes bodies strike with intelligences, instead of bringing objects of the same nature into contact, as in the physical order, i.e., intelligences with intelligences. Finally, let us realize that in the pure idea of motion materiality does not mean a thing: the entire difference between material motion and moral motion consists in the fact that the elements of one are space and time, while time alone is the element of the other; but it is evident that the idea of time alone is enough to give us the idea of motion. Thus, the law of motion is the law of the universality of things, and what we said about physical motion is wholly applicable to intellectual or moral motion.

What should we conclude from all that? That there is not the slightest difficulty in considering the proper activities of man as an *accessory* principle: as a force which works only insofar as it is united with another superior force, just as the force of gravity works only along with the force of initial thrust. Here is the point which we wanted to get at.

Perhaps men will think that there is no place for the philosophy of the ego in this system. This would be a mistake. On the contrary, the philosophy of the ego fits in beautifully with this system: only it is simply reduced to its own true importance, that is all. From what we just said about the double action which rules the world, it does not follow at all that our own activity comes to nothing; this means then that it is very useful for us to meditate on the power which we possess and to strive to understand it as best we can. Man is constantly stimulated by a force, which he does not sense at all, it is true, but this exterior action has an influence upon him by means of his awareness; consequently, no matter how the idea which I find in my head reaches me, I find it there only because I am aware of the idea which I find there. But to become aware is to act. Therefore, I really and unceasingly act at the same time that I am dominated by something more powerful than myself. *I am aware* of it. One factor does not destroy the other, they occur without negating each other, and one is just as demonstrable as the other. So that if someone should ask me how this action operates on me from the outside, this is an entirely different question, and you certainly realize that this is no time to consider it here; a philosophy of higher order has to answer it. Ordinary reason need only show the existence of exterior action and accept it as one of its own fundamental articles of faith; the rest does not concern it. But, who does not know how strange thoughts are introduced into our intelligence? How do we submit ourselves to the advice and opinions of others? What thinking man does not distinctly understand the mechanism of one reason subordinated to another and while it nonetheless preserves all its own power, all its own abilities. Thus, the great problem of free will, no matter how abstruse it may be, would certainly not offer any difficulties, if only men understood how to become permeated with the idea that the nature of intelligent being consists only in awareness and that, insofar as intelligent being is aware, it loses nothing of its own nature, no matter how awareness comes to it.

The point is that the Scottish school,[6] which ruled so long in the philosophical world, confused all questions about ideology. You know that the Scottish school attempts to find the source of all human thought and explain it all by revealing the thread which binds the present perception with the previous perception. Having once come to the source of a certain number of ideas by means of their association, they concluded that all that happens in our intelligence is a product of that same principle cited above, and after that they refused to take anything else into account. Therefore, they imagined that everything can be reduced to the fact of consciousness and upon that fact then empirical psychology was built. But, tell me, is there then anything in the world which we sense more than the incessant production of ideas in our head, a production in which we perform no role? Is there anything that we can be more assured of than this continuous work of our intelligence which takes place without us doing absolutely anything about it? The problem, besides, would not be closer to solution, even if it were possible to trace all our ideas to some single bundle of ideas whose origin would be fully known to us. Certainly in our minds nothing happens which is not linked up in some way or other with what went on before; but it does not follow from this that each change of my thought, each form which my thought takes step by step, is caused by my own power: consequently there is still a place for an immense influence fully distinct from mine. So, at best, empirical theory only verifies certain phenomena in our nature; however, as for the general phenomenon, it does not take that into account at all.

Finally, man's proper activity is genuinely so only when it corresponds to the law. Every time that we act contrary to the law it is no longer we ourselves who determine ourselves, but it is our environment which determines us. When we abandon ourselves to these outside influences, when we go beyond the law, we annihilate ourselves. But in our submission to divine power, we are never fully conscious of this power, therefore, it can never encroach upon our freedom. Thus, our freedom consists only in the fact that we do not sense our dependency: this is enough for us to consider ourselves as perfectly free and liable for everything which we do, for each idea which we think. Unfortunately, man understands freedom in another way: "He believes himself free," says Job, "like a wild baby jackass."[7]

Yes, I am free, how can I doubt it? While I write these lines, do I not know that I have the power not to write them? If a Providence has determined my destiny irrevocably, what difference does it make if I cannot feel its power? But, an idea comes to be associated with that of my liberty, an awesome idea, its terrible, merciless consequence—the misuse of my liberty and *evil* which results from it. Assume that one single molecule of matter would make an arbitrary movement once, for example, instead of tending towards the center of its system, it would deviate a little from the radius in which it is located. What would happen? Would not the whole order of the world be disturbed at once? Would not each atom be moved out of place into infinite space? As if that were not enough, would not all bodies collide together at the opening and destroy one another? Very well, do you realize that each of us does this very same thing each moment in the day? We are constantly making arbitrary movements, and each time we shake the entire universe. And it is not only our exterior movements that cause this awesome devastation within creation but each pulsation of our soul, each of our most intimate thoughts. This is the spectacle which we offer to the Supreme Being. Then why does He stand for this? Why does He not sweep away this world of rebellious creatures? And even more surprising, why has He provided them with this terrible power? He willed it so. "Let us create man in our own image and likeness," He said.[8] This image of God, this likeness with Him—this is our liberty. But as creatures made in such a surprising manner, we are also made so that we may know that we oppose our own creator. Then how is it possible to doubt that, since He decided to give us this surprising power which seems to clash with the whole order of the universe, He did not also decide to give it rules and to let us know how we should use it? In the beginning the whole of humanity personified in one man who represented all future generations heard the Word of God; later on God deigned to illuminate some chosen men, so that they would preserve the truth on earth, and finally, He judged one of us worthy to be invested with all His authority, to be initiated into all His secrets, so that He was *only one* with Him, and charged Him to communicate to us all that we can know about the divine mystery. Here is what sacred doctrine teaches us. But, does our own reason not tell us the same thing? If God were not instructing us, then could the world, we ourselves, or anything else continue to exist for a moment? Would not all be changed immediately into chaos again? This is certainly so, and when our reason does not blind itself by its lying self-confidence, when reason stops immersing itself completely in its pride, then our reason tells us precisely what faith tells us, namely, that God must necessarily instruct and lead man from the very first day of his creation and that He has never ceased and will be ever close to instruct and lead man until the end of time.

Sokolniki, June 30

LETTER V

Much of the soul they talk, but all awry.

Milton[1]

You see, everything leads us back to this absolute principle that human reason itself cannot prescribe a law for itself, any more than human reason could prescribe a law for every other created thing. The law of moral nature has been given to us once and for all, like the law of physical nature: if we find the latter already available, there is not the slightest reason why we should not find the other one already available too. But, like the light from those suns which revolve in other heavens, whose rays though weak nevertheless reach us, the light of the moral law glimmers from a distant and unknown region; it is up to us to keep our eyes open to receive this light when it begins to shine before us. You have seen that we came to these conclusions by way of inductive reasoning which revealed certain elements of identity between the material order and the intellectual order. School psychology[2] proceeds from about the same point, but it does not come to the same conclusions. From natural science it takes only observation, i.e., what is least applicable to the object of its study. Instead of achieving the real unity of

105

things, school psychology only mixes up what should stay eternally separated; instead of discovering law, it discovers chaos. Undoubtedly, an absolute unity exists among all beings: this is the very thing which we are attempting to demonstrate as best we can; furthermore, in that lies the *credo* of every healthy philosophy. But this unity is objective unity, completely outside the reality which we sense; an immense fact which throws an extraordinary light on the great All and forms the logic of cause and effect, but which has nothing in common with the sort of pantheism professed by the majority of contemporary philosophers, a sad teaching which colors all contemporary philosophic systems with its false tint, so that there is no contemporary system which does not end up treating spiritual facts exactly as if they were material, despite all its own pretty promises of spirituality.

The mind by its very nature strives for unity, but unfortunately up to now men still have not really understood in what the real unity of things consists. To convince yourself of this, look at the way in which the majority of intellectuals understand the continuity of the soul. Is it really possible to have an eternal God and a soul, eternal like He, an absolute infinity and another absolute infinity next to it? Is absolute infinity not absolute perfection? How could two eternal beings, two perfect beings exist alongside one another? Here is the whole point: Since there is no legitimate motive for supposing the simultaneous annihilation of both component parts in a being composed of intellect and matter, it was natural for the human mind to arrive at the idea that one of these parts could outlive the other. But at that point the human mind should have called a halt. I may live on a hundred thousand years after this moment, which I call death and which is merely a physical phenomenon having nothing in common with my intellectual being, but this is still far from eternity. And like all man's instinctive ideas, the idea of the immortality of the soul was at first simple and understandable; however, once it had fallen upon the excessively rich soil of the East, it grew inordinately there, and ever-growing it resulted one day in this irreligious dogma which mixes the creature up with the Creator, breaks the line dividing them for all time, burdens the spirit down with the vast weight of a limitless future, and mixes and confuses everything. But afterwards when this idea was introduced into Christianity along with many others inherited from the pagans, it acquired a lot of support from this new force and was thus able to subjugate the heart of man completely. However, it is clear to everyone that the Christian religion considers eternal life as the reward for a perfectly holy life; so, if man still has to merit eternal life, then it is evidently impossible for him to have had it before; if eternal life is simply the reward for a perfect life, how could it be at the end of an existence passed in sin? An astounding thing! Although the human spirit has been illuminated by the greatest of all lights, yet it still is not able to master the whole truth and constantly oscillates between truth and falsehood. One has to admit that every philosophy is necessarily enclosed in a certain fatal circle without any possible exit. In the field of ethics every philosophy makes its own law for itself at the outset and then begins to submit to it without letting us know how or why; in the field of metaphysics every philosophy always sets up a principle in advance, from which it then makes out a whole world of things created by it. So it always begs the question,[3] but this is inevitable: otherwise what function would reason have in all that? None at all, that is evident.

For example, note how the most certain, the most positive, the most strict philosophy of our time proceeds.[4] It begins with the establishment of the fact that, since our reason is the given instrument of knowledge, it is necessary first of all to study how to know our reason. Without that, the philosophy says, there is no way of making suitable usage of reason. After that, this philosophy attempts to dissect and to analyze this reason as best it can. But how does this philosophy perform this preliminary work, this indispensable work, this anatomy of intelligence? Is it not by means of this reason itself? Thus, since in this, its most primary and most important operation, this philosophy is forced to utilize an instrument which by its own admission it still does not know how to use, how can it come to the knowledge which it seeks? This is impossible to understand. However, this is not even everything. More self-confident than all previous philosophical systems, it asserts that it is necessary to treat the spirit absolutely like exterior objects. In that case the very same eye, which you use to see the world, could also allow you to see your very own being. In the same way that you

place the world in front of you, you can place your
own self in front of you; in the same way that you meditate upon the whole world and experiment on it, you
can meditate and experiment upon your own being.
Since the law of identity is common to nature and to
intelligence, you can handle both of them in the same
way. If on the basis of a series of identical phenomena
in the material order, you come to a conclusion about
a general phenomenon in the intellectual order, what
stops you from concluding to a universal fact out of a
series of similar facts by use of the same method? Just
as you are in a position to foresee a physical event,
with the same certitude you can also foresee a moral
fact. The same method used in physics can also be
used in psychology. This is the way empirical philosophy works. Fortunately today this philosophy is
only held individually by some lazy intellectuals who
obstinately continue to stick in their old ruts. A new
light already charts a way through our obscurities,
and everything going on in contemporary philosophy
strives to bring us back to better ways, even this eclec-
ticism[5] which is so gentle and obliging that it seem-
ingly aspires simply for its own self-effacement. Among
the intellectual trends today there is a particular one
which must be distinguished from the others. This is
a type of subtile platonism, a new creation of profound
and meditative Germany; it is transcendent idealism,[6]
filled to overflowing with lofty rational poetry, and it
has already shaken the ancient edifice of philosophical
superstitions to its very foundations. However, up to
now the new creation lives in ethereal heights, where

men can hardly breathe. It hovers in its diaphanous atmosphere either illuminated by some unknown soft and delicate light or else eclipsed in an unclear or dark twilight, so that men take it to be one of those fantastic mirages which occasionally appear in the southern heaven, only to disappear in an instant, without leaving behind any traces in the air or in man's memory. Let us hope that this beautiful and majestic thought will soon descend into inhabitable regions: we will then welcome it with most lively affection. But for the time being let it follow its own vagabond route, and we will continue along a surer route which we have mapped out for ourselves.

So then, if we have conceived of motion in the moral world as well as motion in the physical world as the effect of an initial thrust, then does it not follow from this that both motions are subjected to the same laws in their continuity and, consequently, all intellectual phenomena are simply the result of this analogy? This means that just as bodily collision in nature serves to continue this first thrust, imparted to matter, intellectual collision likewise continues spiritual motion; just as in nature everything is linked with all that goes before it and follows it, so each individual human and each human thought are linked with all human beings and with all human thoughts, those which precede and those which follow; and, since nature is one, so, according to the picturesque expression of Pascal, also *the whole succession of men is one man, who always exists*,[7] and each one of us participates directly in the intellectual work which is being completed throughout the centuries. Finally, just as a certain plastic and perpetual work of the material elements or atoms, i.e., the generation of physical beings, constitutes material nature, so also then a similar work of intellectual elements or ideas, i.e., the generation of spirits, constitutes spiritual nature; and just as I conceive of all tangible matter as one whole, then I must also conceive of the succession of intelligences as a single and sole intelligence.

The main vehicle for the formation of spirits is, of course, the word: without it it is impossible to imagine either the source of intelligence in an individual or his development within humanity. However, the word alone is not enough to produce the great phenomenon of universal intelligence; it is far from being the sole means of communication among men; consequently, it would have to include all the intellectual activity being done in the world. A thousand invisible ties unite the thoughts of one reasonable being with those of another; our most intimate thoughts discover every means possible for reproducing themselves outside; when they are disseminated, when they cross one another, they fuse together, they unite, they pass from one spirit to another, they sow, they fertilize, and finally, they engender universal reason. Sometimes it happens that an idea seems to make no impression upon its surroundings; nonetheless, the movement has been imparted, the impact has taken place; in time the idea will find a congenial thought which the idea will stimulate by its contact, you will see the reincarnation of the idea, and it will produce some surprising effect upon the intellectual world. You know this experi-

111

ment from physics: you hang some balls on a horizontal string, you hold the first ball aside, and it is the last globe which bounds away, the ones in between remain unmoved. Here is how the idea is transmitted through men's brains.* How many great and beautiful thoughts, appearing from somewhere or other, have gripped innumerable multitudes and generations! How many lofty truths live and act, ruling and enlightening us, and no man knows where these formidable powers or brilliant lights come from, nor how they traversed time and space! Cicero said somewhere: "Nature has so formed man's features so that they manifest feelings hidden within our heart: whatever affections we have felt, our eyes always reflect it."⁹ This is completely true; in the intelligent being everything betrays his intimate thought; the whole man is completely communicated to his neighbor, and in this way intelligences are engendered. For intelligence does not come into being any more miraculously than anything else; it is a generation like any other. One and the same law presides over every reproduction, whatever its nature be; nothing is engendered except by contact or fusion of beings; no force, no power, acts in an isolated manner. We need only note that the very fact of generation takes place somewhere outside of our direct perception. Thus, just as in the physical world you observe

* It is known that the famous proof for the existence of God, ascribed to Descartes, was invented by Anselm, who lived in the eleventh century. The proof remained buried in a corner of the human spirit for almost five hundred years, until Descartes came and handed it over to philosophy.⁸

the effects of different natural forces—such as attraction, assimilation, affinity—but, in the final analysis, you come to an incomprehensible fact, the act which confers physical life, so also in the intellectual world we clearly see the effects of different human powers; however, we definitively come to something which escapes our immediate perception, the act which confers intellectual life.

But what is this universal intelligence which corresponds to universal matter and in which moral phenomena occur similarly to the way in which the phenomena of the physical order occur within materiality? It is nothing but the sum of all the ideas which live on in man's memory. In order to become the patrimony of mankind, the idea must go through a certain number of generations; in other words, the idea falls under the domain of universal reason only in the state of tradition. But here we are not at all referring only to these traditions which history and science furnish the human spirit and which form only a part of universal memory. There are also many ideas which have never been announced before public meetings, have never been sung by rhapsodists, have never been marked either on columns or on parchments; the dates of their appearance have never been ascertained by calculation or by the course of the stars, criticism has never weighed them on its partial balance, but an unknown hand puts them into the interior of souls; the first smile of the mother, the first caress of the father, communicates them to the heart of the newborn. These are the powerful recollections in which the experience of the ages is concentrated: each individual receives them with the air which he breathes. In this milieu, then, all the wonders of intelligence are completed. Undoubtedly, this hidden experience of the centuries does not reach each part of mankind in a complete way; nonetheless, it forms the intellectual substance of the universe, this hidden experience flows in the blood of the human races, it is incorporated with their fibre, and finally it continues those other more mysterious traditions, without origins on earth, which serve as the basis for all societies. It is a known fact that in each tribe, no matter how isolated it has been from the great universal movement, there is always a certain number of more or less exact notions about Supreme Being, about good and evil, about what is just and what is unjust. Without these notions the tribe could not subsist any more than without the base food-products from the soil on which it is grouped and the trees which give it shelter. Where do these notions come from? No one knows; traditions, that is all; there is no way of getting back to their origin: children learned them from their fathers and mothers—that is their entire genealogy. Then the centuries come to descend upon these primitive ideas, experience accumulates upon them, science is founded upon them, and on this invisible basis the human spirit develops. And here then, by means of factual data, we come to the very same point where reasoning leads up to this initial thrust, without which, as we have seen, nothing would move in nature and which is just as necessary here as there.

And tell me please, can you conceive of an intelligent being without any kind of an idea? Can you imagine reason in man before he has made use of it? Can you imagine something in the head of a child before he has been taught by those who assisted at his entry into life? Men have seen squat children among forest beasts, whose traits these children adopted, later recover their mental faculties, but these children had not been abandoned from the first days of their existence. The offspring of the most robust animal would inevitably perish, if it were left behind by the female immediately after birth; man, the weakest of all animals, since he requires breast-feeding for six or seven months and his cranium is without bone-protection for several days after birth, could not possibly live through the first stage of life without the security of a mother's hands. This means that these children received the intellectual seed before they were separated from their parents. If a man were separated from his parents and from every human being from the moment he opened his eyes to the light, if he were not to perceive the glance of a being similar to himself even once and not to hear even a single sound of his voice, and if he were to live on this way up to the age of reason, I guarantee that he would not be different from the mammals which the naturalist places in that same category. Is there anything more absurd than the supposition that each human individual begins his species anew, like the beast? But nonetheless, that is the hypothesis which serves as the basis for an entire ideological construction. They assume that this tiny unformed being, still connected by the umbilical cord to the uterus of the mother, is an intelligent being. But how do they know this? Is it by this galvanic action which causes the child to jump about that you recognize the heavenly gift bestowed upon him? Or is it in this stupid glance, in these tears, in this penetrating cry that you discovered the being created in the image of God? Will he, I ask you, ever have an idea which will not have come to him from the small number of notions placed in his brain by his mother, his nurse, or another human creature during the first days of his existence? The first man was no crying child, but a complete man, therefore, he was fully able to resemble God and really did resemble Him: however, certainly it is not the human embryo which is made in the image of God. The real nature of man consists in the fact that he is the only being capable of receiving an infinite teaching; in this then lies his greatness, his superiority over all creatures. But for him to raise himself up to the condition of an intelligent being, a ray from supreme reason must illuminate his brain. On the day when man was created God spoke with him, and man heard and understood Him: this is the true genesis of human reason; psychology will never find a more profound explanation. Later, he partially lost the ability to hear the voice of God; this was a natural consequence of the gift of unlimited liberty which he had obtained. But he did not lose his recollections of God's first words which resounded in his ear. Then this same word from God, addressed to the first man and transmitted from generation to generation, strikes the child in the crib and introduces him into the intellectual world and really makes him into a thinking being. The same method which God used in order to create man from nothing, He utilizes today in order to create every new thinking being. It is always God who speaks to man through the intermediary of his fellow men.

In that case, the idea of the human being coming into the world with completed intelligence does not have, as you see, any foundation at all either in experience or in abstraction. The great law of the constant and direct influence of a supreme principle is simply reproduced in the general life of man, as it is reproduced in all creation. There it is a force contained in a *quantity,* here it is a principle contained in a *tradition;* but it is always the same fact of an exterior influence acting upon the being, no matter what it be, first instantaneously and then in a continuous and permanent manner.

No matter how much we retreat within ourselves, no matter how much we rummage within the most secret depths of our heart, we shall never find anything there other than the thoughts inherited from our ancestors on earth. This understanding, which men analyze and break into pieces, will always remain simply the understanding of all the generations which succeeded one another from the first man down to us; and when we meditate upon the capabilities of our mind, we simply utilize this same universal reason, for better or worse, in order to observe the part of it which we received in the course of our personal existence. Is that a faculty of the soul? It is an idea, an idea which we find already present in our own mind, without knowing how it

117

came into our mind, and it in turn provokes another. However, in your opinion, where could the first idea come from, if not from this ocean of ideas in which we swim? If we were deprived of contact with other intelligent beings, we would eat grass instead of speculating on our nature. If men do not agree that the thought of man is the thought of mankind, then there is no way to understand what it is. As in the rest of the created world, so in the intellectual world nothing can be understood as perfectly isolated, as if it were self-sufficient. And, finally, if it is true that in the higher or *objective* reality, man's reason is really only the perpetual reproduction of God's thought, then it is also certain that his present reason or *subjective* reason is only the reason made by man's reason itself thanks to his free will. It is true that the school does not make any room for all that; there exists only one single and unique reason for the school: the given man is man just as he came forth from the hands of the Creator; created free, he did not misuse his freedom; a voluntary being, he remained the same as inert objects, obedient to an irresistible force; the innumerable errors, the coarse superstitions, generated by him, the crimes with which he soiled himself, nothing of all that left traces on his soul. There he is just as he was on the day when God's breath animated his worldly existence, just as pure, just as chaste, as then, when nothing had polluted his young nature; to the school man is always the same; he was the same at all times, he is the same in all places; as we are so we should be; and this mass of incomplete, fantastic, incoherent thoughts, which we call the human mind, is pure intelligence, the heavenly emanation flowing from God Himself, according to the school; nothing has changed it, nothing has touched it. That is human wisdom.

Nevertheless, the human spirit has always felt the need of reconstituting itself according to an ideal image. Up to the moment of the appearance of Christianity, the human spirit simply did nothing but work on this image which constantly escaped it and which it constantly reworked; this was the great task of antiquity. And man was naturally reduced at that time to seeking the image in himself. But it is surprising that even in our day philosophy, with the highest teachings offered by Christianity before it, still sometimes remains obstinately in the circle in which the ancient world was confined and does not think to look for the model of perfect intelligence somewhere outside of human nature, by turning, for example, towards the sublime doctrine destined to preserve the oldest traditions of the world among men, or towards this admirable book which so clearly carries the stamp of absolute reason, i.e., this very same reason which the human spirit seeks and cannot find. Just meditate a little in an honest way about the system which has been revealed and you will be astounded by the great expression of intellectual perfection which dominates it completely; you will see that all the outstanding minds which you meet there simply form part of one sole vast mind which fills and permeates this world, in which the past, the present, and the future form only one indivisible whole; you will feel that there every-

119

thing aims at making you understand the nature of a reason which is not subordinated to the conditions of time and space and which man once possessed, which he lost, which he will find again one day, and which was manifested to us in the person of Christ. Note that on this question philosophical spirituality[10] does not differ at all from the opposite system,[11] because it is all the same if men hold that human understanding is a *tabula rasa,* in accordance with the old adage of the empirical school, "There is nothing in the mind which is not first in the senses," or if they assume that human understanding acts by means of its own power and repeat with Descartes, "I shut out all my senses and I live";[12] in both cases we always deal with the reason which we find in ourselves today, but not with the reason which was given as a present to us in the beginning; therefore, we could never investigate the genuine spiritual principle at all, but this distorted, disfigured principle, perverted by man's arbitrariness.

Besides, assuredly the most profound and most productive of all the known systems is the one which strives to construct conscientiously an absolutely abstract intelligence, an exclusively intelligent nature, in order to take the intellectual phenomenon into account without going back to the very source of the spiritual principle. But, since it is always man in his present state who furnishes the materials from which this system constructs its model, it happens that this system shows us artificial reason again, but not original reason. The profound thinker,[13] the author of this philosophy, did not see that there was no point in representing an intelligence which would only will to seek out and evoke supreme intelligence; an intelligence with a mode of perfectly legitimate activity, as everything which exists, and intelligence whose power would consist only in an infinite tendency to fuse with this other intelligence. If he had started out with that premise, he would have certainly come to the idea of a genuinely pure reason, because reason would have become a simple reflection of absolute reason and the analysis of this reason would have doubtless led him to conclusions of vast importance, and over and above this he would not have fallen into the false teaching about the *autonomy* of human reason, about some certain imperative law, which exists within our reason itself and gives it the ability to rise up by its own power to the whole fullness of the perfection attainable by it, finally another, even more arrogant philosophy, the philosophy of *the omnipotence of the human ego*[14] would not have owed it its own existence.

However, even so, this philosopher should be treated justly: as is, his creation merits complete respect. We owe all the healthy ideas in the world today to the movement which he gave to philosophical knowledge; and we ourselves are nothing but a logical consequence of his idea. He traced the limits of human reason with steadfast hand; he made it clear that reason had to accept its two most profound convictions without being able to prove them, namely: the existence of God and the unlimited continuity of its own being; he taught us that a supreme logic exists, which cannot be fitted under our measurements and which is imposed upon us despite ourselves, and that there is a world which is contemporary and different from the one on which we move and that our reason must recognize this world, because of the opposite danger of falling into nothingness, and that from this we should draw all our knowledge, in order then to adapt our knowledge to the real world. But after all, one has to agree that his mission[15] was simply to indicate a new route for philosophy and that if he performed great services for the human spirit it was only in the sense that he forced the human spirit to return back along its road.

In summarizing the results of the study, which we have just made, we arrive at the following: all that exists in the world of ideas comes from a certain number of notions which have been transmitted traditionally, and which do not belong to any intellectual individual any more than the forces of nature belong to any physical individual. *Archetypes* of Plato, *innate ideas* of Descartes, *a priori* of Kant, all these diverse elements of thought, which were necessarily recognized by all profound thinkers as in advance of any kind of operation by the soul, as preceding all experimental knowledge and all the appropriate activity of the mind, all these pre-existing seeds of reason without which man would simply be a two-legged and two-armed mammal—no more, no less, and this notwithstanding the great span of his facial angle, nor the volume of his skull, nor the vertical posture of his body —are summed up in the ideas which come to us from the intellectuals who preceded us in life and those who have been charged with the task of introducing us to our personal existence. Infused miraculously into the mind of the first human being on the day of his creation by the same hand which directed the planets upon their elliptical orbits, made inert matter move, and gave life to organic being—these, then, are the ideas which make the intelligence move and push man into the vast circle in which he is meant to travel. Arising as a consequence of the reciprocal contact of spirits and by reason of a mysterious principle which perpetuates the influence of supreme intelligence upon created intelligence, these ideas cause intellectual nature to continue to exist in the same way that a similar contact and an analogous principle causes material nature to continue to exist. Thus, the original thrust continues in all things, and thus it is definitively molded into a constant and immediate providence, which extends its influence upon the whole universality of being.

Once this is established, the study that we still have to do is simple: we only have to investigate the movement of these traditions throughout the history of humanity, in order to see how and where the idea, originally put into the heart of man, was preserved in its wholeness and purity.

LETTER VI

The question may be asked why so many men cultivated the practical and the fine arts amid so many shocks, civil wars, conspiracies, crimes, and inanities in Italy and then in the other Christian states; that is something we do not see under the domination of the Turks.

Voltaire. *Essay on Customs*[1]

Madame,

You have seen in my preceding letters how important it is to understand the movement of thought throughout the passing of the ages. But you should also have seen that, when one becomes permeated with the fundamental idea that there is no truth in man's mind other than that which God deposited there with His own Hand when He made man out of nothing, then it becomes impossible to view the movement of the centuries in the same way in which popular history is viewed. For it is found that not only a providence or a perfectly wise intellect presides over the course of events but even an immediate and constant influence of this providence or of this reason upon man's spirit is discernible. If it is once admitted that, in order to be set in motion, the reason of created being originally had to receive an impulse which did not come from its own nature and that its initial ideas, its initial knowledge, could only have been miraculous communications of supreme reason, it follows that during the

124

course of the progress of human reason the force which constituted it in this way must have continued to exercise upon it the same influence which the force utilized at the moment when it imparted its first movement to human reason.

This way of understanding intelligent being in history and its progress must have become familiar to you, Madame, if you fully grasped the things which we agreed upon previously. You have seen that pure, metaphysical reasoning perfectly demonstrates the perpetuity of an exterior influence upon the mind of man. But it is not necessary to have recourse to metaphysics; the conclusion must follow all by itself; it cannot be denied without denying the premises from which it is drawn. So, if man reflects upon the very mode of this continuous influence of divine reason in the moral world, he will find, as we have just seen, that divine reason alone is necessarily consistent with its initial influence and must still take place in such a way as not to destroy the liberty of human reason, nor render the proper activity of reason useless. Thus, there is nothing surprising in the fact that there was a people who had preserved the tradition of God's initial communications in a purer and more definite manner than others and that from time to time men appeared in whom the primitive fact of the moral order was renewed. Remove this people, remove these privileged men and it would be necessary to suppose that divine thought was revealed just as fully and vividly to all people in all epochs within the universal life of man. You realize that this would result in the destruction of all individuality and all freedom in the world: this would mean the annihilation of the given object. It is evident that individuality and freedom exist only insofar as there is diversity of intelligence, moral powers, and knowledge. Instead of supposing that an extraordinary degree of submission to primitive traditions or a particular capacity for understanding the truth originally infused into the human spirit exists in a nation or in some isolated spirits supposedly charged with guarding this gift, all that one need do is to admit a moral fact perfectly analogous to what takes place incessantly before our eyes, namely, the knowledge that some peoples and individuals are in possession of certain intuitions which other peoples and individuals do not enjoy.

Among the rest of humanity these great traditions are also maintained with more or less purity according to the different situations of the people; and man advanced on the path traced out for him only by the torchlight of these powerful truths which a reason other than his own engendered in his intellect. But there was only one source of light upon earth. This source did not indeed burn like human knowledge, it did not dispense a deceiving burst of light; concentrated at one point, luminous and invisible at one and the same time, like all the world's great mysteries, ardent but hidden like the fire of life, everything was illuminated by this inexpressible light, and everything tended towards this common center, while everything seemed to shine by its luster and to be directed towards the most opposite goals.* But when the time of the great catastrophe in the intellectual world arrived, all man's vainly-created powers disappeared at once and amid the general conflagration only the sole tabernacle of eternal truth remained standing. That is how the unity of history should be understood, and that is how this idea elevates itself to the level of a genuine philosophy of time, which evinces intellectual being just as subordinate to a general and absolute law as the rest of creation.

Madame, I would like you to be able to achieve this abstract and religious manner of sensing history; for nothing enlarges our thought and purges our soul as these insights, however obscure, into a providence which dominates the centuries and leads humanity to its final destinies. But meanwhile, let us try to form a philosophy of history which may at least shed some light upon the vast region of human memories, a light like the bright dawning of day for us. We shall profit all the more from this preparatory study of history, since it in itself can supply us with a complete system which could, if necessary, satisfy us, if by chance something happens to halt our subsequent progress. Moreover, please remember, Madame, that I am not addressing you from the pulpit and that these letters

---

* It is not necessary to attempt to determine geographically the point on earth upon which this source of enlightenment existed; but one thing is certain—the traditions of all people on earth converge with the result that incipient human knowledge comes from the same regions of the globe.

are simply the continuation of our interrupted con-
versations which provided me with so many sweet
moments and which, I enjoy reiterating, were means
of genuine consolation for me at a time when I had
great need of them. Do not expect to find me more
didactic than usual this time; be prepared to contribute something of your own to this meditation.

You have undoubtedly already noticed that the present inclination of the human spirit is evidently aimed
at giving every type of knowledge an historical form.
In meditations upon the philosophical foundations of
historical thought, men cannot fail to recognize that
today history is called upon to achieve an importance
infinitely higher than it has had up to now. It may be
said that today the human spirit thrives only on history, that the human spirit keeps turning incessantly
back to the past and continually tries to gain new
strength by relating it to its memories, the contemplation of its past development, the study of the forces
which regulated and directed its advance throughout
the centuries. This change in the attitude of modern
science is certainly a very fortunate one. It is time to
realize that human reason is not simply constituted by
the force which it has in the narrow present, but that
there is another force in it which, by integrating both
past and future into a single thought, forms its true
being and places it in its genuine sphere of activity.

But, Madame, do you not find, in general, that traditional or narrative history is necessarily incomplete?
Is it not true that this history always contains only
what man's memory retains? But it does not retain all

that happens in the world. So, the present historical point of view could not satisfy reason, since it proves nothing. Despite the philosophical spirit which has permeated history in our day, the useful works of criticism and the help which the natural sciences, astronomy, geology and even genuine physics, have lent to history lately, nonetheless, as you see, history has still not been able to attain either *unity* or this lofty morality which would be derived from a distinct insight into the general law within moral, historical movement. The human spirit has always strived towards this great goal in its contemplation of past centuries, but, as for the superficial lessons otherwise drawn from history, these lessons of banal philosophy, these examples of some sort of virtue—as if virtue were displayed upon the world's great theatre, as if the essential traits of virtue were not directed at remaining hidden—this trivial psychological morality of history[2] which has never made a single honest man but a host of scoundrels and fools of all types and which only serves to perpetuate the world's miserable comedy—all that has diverted reason away from the genuine lessons which human traditions ought to provide. As long as the Christian religious spirit dominated science, a profound thought, even though badly articulated, communicated something of its original holy inspiration to these studies. But at this epoch historical criticism was still so incomplete, so many facts, especially those from primitive times, were still preserved within humanity's memory in so disfigured a manner that all the religious lights were incapable of dispersing this profound darkness, and history, though illuminated by superior enlightenment, did not advance in any less a mundane manner. Today a rational way of envisaging history should undoubtedly produce a perfectly positive result. The spirit of our century demands an entirely new philosophy of history which would not resemble the present philosophy of history any more than the learned analyses of astronomy today resemble the series of gnomic observations by Hipparchus and the rest of the ancient astronomers. However, men must realize that there will never be enough facts to demonstrate everything and that we have enough of them to enable us to presage many things since the times of Moses and Herodotus. No matter what sort of factual compilation men may make, these will never lead to certitude; certitude can only result from the way in which the facts are understood. So, for example, the experimentation of centuries, which had taught Kepler the laws of planetary motion, was not enough to reveal the general law of nature to him; this discovery[3] was reserved to a kind of extraordinary revelation, a pious meditation. Madame, that is the history which we must try to understand.

First of all, what is the significance of these rapprochements between centuries and nations, hoarded up by vain erudition? Is it all these linguistic, ethnic, and intellectual genealogies? Will not a blind and obstinate philosophy[4] always clear them out of the way by its old argument about the general uniformity of human nature? Will it not deny all these marvelous interrelationships of the times by using its favorite theory, i.e., the natural development of the human spirit without any traces of providence, without any cause other than the mechanic force of its own nature? This philosophy considers the human spirit nothing more than a snowball which grows by rolling, that is all. Besides, from its own point of view this philosophy either sees progress and a natural perfection everywhere as something inherent in human nature or else simply finds a motiveless, meaningless movement.

Depending upon the different intellectual traits, whether somber and hopeless or else hopeful and amenable, this philosophy either sees man simply fluttering about imbecilely like a fly in the sun, or else rising and always advancing thanks to his sublime nature, but it is always man and nothing but man. This willfully ignorant philosophy learns nothing from the physical world which it imagines that it knows, except what is offered to the vain curiosity of the mind and the senses; the great streams of light which this world gives off never reach this philosophy and finally, even if it should decide upon the acknowledgement of a plan, a design, or a reason in the totality of things, the submission of human intelligence to it, and the acceptance of all the consequences resulting from it with reference to the phenomena of universal moral order, such a task remains impossible as long as this philosophy is what it is. Thus, there is no point either in linking up the times or in working perpetually upon factual material: men must try to characterize the great epochs in history from a moral viewpoint and attempt to determine the traits of each age with perfect impartiality in accordance with the law of a lofty practical reason. Moreover, if men pay strict attention to this, they will find that historical data has been completed, people have recited all their traditions, and if one day past epochs may be clarified in better fashion, here again it will occur not by means of this critical method, which is only capable of digging up the old ashes of people, but rather by means of some purely rational procedure; as for real facts, there are no more of them to be found. *The sole task of history today consists in meditating.*

If we admit this, history would fit naturally into the general system of philosophy and would henceforth form an integral part of it. A number of things which would be left to novelists and poets would then, of course, be severed from history. But there would still be much which would surge up from the nebulous atmosphere in which it still lies, in order to be put at the most evident heights of the new system. These things would no longer receive their character of truth uniquely from the chronicle, but henceforth moral reasoning would imprint the stamp of certitude upon them in the same way that geometric reasoning reduced to formulae and to articles of faith these axioms of natural philosophy which were discovered by experience and observation. For example, that would be the case with reference to the epoch still so misunderstood, not because of any absence of data or monuments, but because of an absence of thought; I mean the first centuries of our Christian era in which all history culminates, in which everything terminates and begins, and it can be said, without fear of exaggeration, that humanity's entire past is intermingled with all of its future in that period.

There will come a day when historical thought will no longer be able to remain indifferent in the face of this imposing spectacle made up of the initial greatness of men reduced to dust, as well as all the future greatness contained within it. This is also the case with reference to the long period which followed and continued this age of mankind's regeneration, a period so misrepresented not long ago by philosophic prejudice and fanaticism; then such lively lights were concealed in the depths of the most opaque darkness, then such prodigious moral forces were preserved and flourished amid the apparent intellectual immobility, and we have begun to understand this only since the human spirit has taken a new turn.

In this way then this period may be seen in all its admirable reality and with all its great teaching. Then gigantic figures, lost in the crowd of historical personalities at this moment, would walk out from the shadow which envelops them, whereas many renowned characters, lavishly venerated by men for a long time in a criminal or imbecilic fashion, would fall forever into oblivion. For example, this would be the case with respect to the new fate of some biblical personalities, misunderstood or neglected by human reason, and that of some pagan sages whom human reason surrounded with more glory than they deserved. Take Moses and Socrates, for example. Men would grasp once and for all that the former gave the true God to men, whereas the latter simply bequeathed them pusillanimous and disquieting doubt. As for David and Marcus Aurelius, the former is the perfect model of very holy heroism, whereas the latter is basically simply a curious example of artificial greatness and pompous virtue. Men would no longer remember Cato tearing out his entrails except as a means of justly evaluating the philosophy which inspired this furious virtue and miserable greatness in man. I believe that amid the glories of paganism Epicurus' name would be freed from ₊the prejudice which blemished it and new interest would be attached to his historical position.

Other great notables would suffer a new lot in the same way. The Stagirite's name,[5] for example, would be pronounced henceforth only with a kind of abhorrence, and Mohammed's, with profound respect. The former would be considered as an angel of darkness who repressed all the forces for good in mankind during a number of centuries; the latter as a beneficent being, one of those who contributed the most towards the realization of the plan conceived of by *divine wisdom* for the salvation of mankind. Finally, I have to tell you that a sort of infamy would become linked with Homer's name. Plato's judgment upon this corruptor of man, motivated as it was by his religious instinct, would not longer be viewed as one of his famous utopian sallies, but rather as one of his admirable anticipations of future thought. One day men must learn to blush upon recalling this guilty enchanter who contributed to the degradation of human nature in such a terrible way; men must sorrowfully

make repentance for the incense which they have lavished upon this flatterer of their vilest passions, this
man who soiled the sacred tradition of truth and filled
men's hearts with filth in order to please. All these
ideas which remain more or less lifeless in some independent brains would henceforth be irrevocably set
in the moral feeling of humanity and would become
much like axioms of common sense.

But in this sense, one of the most important lessons
to be derived from history would consist in imbedding
within humanity's memory the respective ranks of
people who have disappeared from the world and in
filling living people's consciousness with a sense of
their particular mission. Each nation should perceive
its present actual existence through a clear understanding of the different epochs in its past life and should
be able to predict somewhat the course of its own
future development. In this way, the people's genuine
national consciousness would be composed of a certain
number of positive ideas, evident truths deduced from
their recollections, strong convictions which would
more or less dominate all their minds and would urge
them along towards a similar goal. In that case the
nationality groups, which have simply divided men
up to now, would combine with one another in order
to produce one harmonic and universal result, since
they would be divested of their blindness and their
impassioned interest; then all people would link arms
and march together towards a single goal.

I know that our wise men have promised this intellectual coalescence to philosophy and to the progress

of universal enlightenment; however, if men reflect upon the fact that the people, though composite beings, are nonetheless truly moral beings just as individuals are and that, as a result, a similar law presides over the intellectual life of both, then it will be seen that *the activity of the great human families necessarily depends upon this personal feeling which causes them to conceive of themselves as separate from the rest of humanity with their own unique existence and individual interest. This feeling is a necessary element of world consciousness and constitutes, so to say, the ego of the collective human being.* Therefore, in our hopes for future happiness and indefinite perfection we could not initially isolate the great individual nationalities any more than their less important composite parts. We must accept them as principles and means for reaching a perfect state.

Thus, the cosmopolitan future of philosophy is only an idle dream. First, men must concentrate upon drawing up a set of domestic morals different from their political morality; people have to learn how to know themselves first and how to evaluate themselves just as individuals, so that they may recognize their own vices and virtues; so that they may learn to admit the faults and the crimes which they have committed, and repair the evil which they have done, or else to persevere upon the good path which they are following. Those are the inevitable moral conditions leading to genuine perfectibility for the masses, just as for individuals; in order to fulfill their destinies in the world, both have to look back upon their past lives and discover their future in the past.

So you see that historical criticism would no longer be reduced to satisfying vain curiosity but would become the most august of magistrates. It would exercise implacable justice upon illustriousness and greatness in every century, scrutinize all the famous men of glory, explain every phantom and every historical illusion, and would concentrate upon destroying the false images encumbering man's memory, so that reason could deduce certain consequences for the present from the past, made accessible to reason in its true light, and could look into the infinite expanses of the future.

I believe then that an immense glory, the glory of Greece, would almost completely pass away; I believe that a day will come when man's moral thinking will become permeated simply by a holy sadness for this deceptive and illusory earth from which the genius of deceit disseminated seduction and falsehood upon the rest of the world for such a long time. No longer would the pure soul of a Fénelon[6] be seen nourishing itself indolently upon voluptuous images created by the most frightful depravation that ever befell the human spirit, nor would powerful intellectuals allow themselves to be overpowered by sensual inspirations from Plato;* but, in contrast to this, the old, almost forgotten thoughts of some religious minds would come into their own, namely those powerful thinkers and genuine heroes of thought who indicated with one hand the path which society should pursue at the dawn of the new society, while with the other hand they fought

* Schleiermacher, Schelling, Cousin, etc.

against the agonizing monster of polytheism; the prodigious conceptions of these wise men, to whom God had committed the preservation of His first Words admirably and unexpectedly applicable to society. And in the unique visions of the future granted to some chosen men people would begin to note in particular the basic, conscious manifestation of the absolute interrelationship between historic periods, as well as the fact that the prophecies do not really refer *to any definite epoch* but are lessons referring indiscriminately to all historical periods. Moreover, men would find that all you have to do is to look around yourself, as it were, in order to see their perpetual fulfillment taking place within the successive phases of society as the daily, luminous manifestations of the eternal law in the moral world, in such a way that the reality of prophecy would thus become as palpable as the very reality of the events which carry us onward.*

Finally, here is the most important lesson that history should impart to us, and within our system, in helping us to understand this universal life of intelligent being, which alone can provide the answer to the *human enigma*, this lesson epitomizes the entire philosophy of history: instead of being satisfied with the meaningless system of the *mechanical* perfection of his

* For example, men will no longer look for great Babylon in any specific earthly dominion, as they did in former times; they will sense it living amid the crash of its collapse, i.e., men will realize that the sublime historian of the future[7] who related this horrible fall was not thinking about any particular empire at all but about the collapse of all materialistic societies in the present and future.

nature, so manifestly contradicted by the experience of all the centuries, man should realize that, when abandoned, he himself has never advanced except towards an indefinite degradation. Though from time to time there have been progressive epochs among all people and lucid moments in man's universal life, sublime flashes of reason, prodigious efforts of man's nature—which is true—yet there is no proof of any permanent and continuous advancement of society in general, and only in the society of which we are members, namely, the Christian society, which was not made by men's hands, can one perceive a genuine, ascending movement and a real principle of true progress. We have doubtless assimilated what the spirit of the ancients imagined or discovered before us; we have made use of it and in this way reforged the broken link in the great historical chain, but it does not follow that people would have reached this present stage of development without the wholly spontaneous and unique historical phenomenon[8] which was outside of the usual generation of human ideas, wholly unrelated to any natural chain of events, and which separates the ancient world from the new world.

Thereafter, Madame, would the wise man look upon the past, back to the movement when a supernatural power imparted an entirely new movement upon the human spirit, and his imagination would recall the world in its true light as corrupt, bloody, and false. The wise man would then recognize that the progress of people and generations, which he had so admired, had really led simply to a brutishness infinitely below that of people whom we call savages and he would thus realize clearly how imperfect the civilizations of the ancient world were; he would see that there was no principle of continuity and permanence in them. He would say to himself: Profound Egyptian wisdom, charming Ionian art, austere Roman virtues, dazzling Alexandrian magnificence, what has become of you? You brilliant civilizations, as old as the world, nurtured by all the powers on earth, associated in every glory, greatness, and domination in the world, and finally linked to the most enormous power[9] which ever weighed down upon the earth with its world empire, how could you have been annihilated?* What did all this work of centuries mean then, all these superb efforts of intelligent nature, if new people who had not participated in it in any way were one day to destroy all of it, raze this magnificent edifice, and plough upon its *ruins*! Had man built that only to see all his own work reduced to dust one day? Had he accumulated so much only to lose it all in one day? Had he risen so high only to fall even lower than his initial state?

But do not be mistaken about it, Madame, it was not the barbarians who destroyed the ancient world; it was already a stinking cadaver; the barbarians simply tossed its dust into the wind. Before this occurrence, these same barbarians had attacked the ancient societies without being able to subdue them; history scarcely remembers their first invasions. The truth is that the principle of life which had supported human

* Alexander, Seleucides, Marcus-Aurelius, Julian, Lagides, etc., etc.

society up to that time was exhausted, and the material interest, or, if you prefer, the real interest which had until then solely determined the social movement had, so to say, completed its task and had concluded the preliminary education of mankind. For, no matter how much human thought tries to quit its terrestrial sphere, it can only raise itself up from time to time to the superior regions in which the genuine principle of social life is to be found, and, as a result, human thought can never give society its definitive stability. The entire history which I am relating to you is contained in this truth.

Unfortunately men have habitually seen only separated states in Europe for too long a time. As a result, the stability of the new society and its immense superiority over the ancient one could not be fully appreciated. Men overlooked the fact that for a number of centuries this society formed a genuine federal system, or rather a single people, and that this system was dissolved only by the Reformation. But when the Reformation came, the society had already been completely constructed for eternity. Before this deplorable event European people considered themselves as part of one single social body, geographically divided into different states, but morally united as one. For a long time they had no public law other than the decrees of the church; the wars being waged then were regarded as domestic wars; a sole, unique interest animated this entire world, a sole thought inspired it. That is what makes the history of the Middle Ages so profoundly philosophical; it is literally the history of the human spirit. The moral movement, the movement of thought accomplished everything; purely political events always occupied only a secondary place in the whole picture, and this can be proved precisely by these religious wars which the philosophy of the past century found so horrifying. Voltaire correctly remarks that religious convictions have caused wars only among Christians,[10] and then he proceeds to talk nonsense in his usual way. However, when you discover a unique fact in history, it is worth trying to understand what produced it and what resulted from it. Tell me, could the reign of thought be established on earth in any way other than by imparting to this principle of thought all its reality, all its intensity? The appearance of things has changed, to be sure, but this is the result of the schism; in shattering the unity of thought, it also shattered the unity of society, but the foundation is certainly the same; Europe is still Christendom, no matter what it does. Europe will certainly never return to the historical state of its age of youth and faith, but there is also no doubt that one day the lines which separate Christian people will be obliterated once again and that the original principle of modern society will become manifest more energetically than ever under a new form. This is an article of faith for a Christian; he is not permitted to doubt about this future, any more than about the past upon which his faith is founded; why, it is a proven fact to every halfway serious intellectual. Who knows whether this day is not closer than men think? Today there certainly is a religious movement at work deep within men's souls, there are changes in the march of science, the supreme power in this century, and from time to time something solemn and contemplative is noticeable within men's souls. Who knows, these may be the harbingers of some great moral and social phenomena which will lead to a general revolution among intelligent beings, whereby articles of faith which are now simply part of man's promised destiny would become probabilities, certitudes belonging to universal reason.

The way to study the special characteristics of the new society is to concentrate upon this great family of Christian people, European society. There you will find the elements of stability and genuine progress, which set it apart from every other social system in the world; all that we can learn from history is concealed right there. Thus, we can see that despite all the revolutions which took place in modern society, it has not lost any of its vitality—in fact, every day it grows in strength, every day we notice new progressive forces which are even stronger than those which developed initially within it. For example, the Arabs, the Tatars, and the Turks were not only incapable of destroying it, but they even helped to consolidate it. You know that these first two nations attacked Europe before the invention of cannon-powder, which proves that it is not guns which have preserved Europe from destruction. At the same time one of these people invaded the two societies which survived from the ancient world, namely India and China. It is true that these two societies also did not perish, thanks to their immense populations, the inert yet reactionary masses, but their natural uniqueness was lost, the old, life-giving principle was driven out to the extremities of their social body, with the result that the death sentence was every bit as definite in their case.

The spectacle offered by India and China today should provide us with an important lesson. For, by studying them, we become, as it were, contemporaries to a world which has left only some dust around us for us to look at. Thus, we can learn what would have become of humanity without the new impetus imparted to it elsewhere by an omnipotent hand. And notice, since time immemorial China apparently possessed the three great instruments which have, so men say, done the most to accelerate the progress of the human spirit in our lands: the compass, the printing-press and cannon-powder. Well, what good were they? Did the Chinese circumnavigate the globe? Did they discover a new hemisphere? Do they possess a literature more vast than the one we had before the invention of printing? Have they had Fredericks and Bonapartes in the deadly art of war, as we have had? For proof of the impotency and miserable condition inherent in every society not founded upon the truth immediately issuing from supreme reason, do we need to look any further than the abject state to which India was reduced by conquest, first by the Tatars and then by the English? I am personally convinced that this dull Chinese immobility and this extraordinary degradation of the Indian people, the standard-bearers of the most ancient natural knowledge and of the germs for all the human sciences, provides us with a specific lesson and that this is why God preserved them upon earth.*

Madame, you have often heard men *attribute* the fall of the Roman empire to moral decay and the despotism resulting from it. However, in this universal upheaval, it is not only Rome that fell; the entire ancient civilization collapsed. The Egypt of the Pharoahs, the Greece of Pericles, the second Egypt of Lagides, and the whole Hellenic empire of Alexander which extended beyond the Indus river, finally, Judaism itself after it became Hellenized—all that was fused in the Roman masses and formed one single piece, one unique society which represented all previous generations since creation and contained all the moral and intellectual powers developed in human nature up to that time. Then it is not simply an empire which fell; human society was annihilated and began

---

* Could it not be the effect of this law, which we see influencing the individual each day, applied to the collective intelligence of people: namely, that any reasoning process having taken, for some reason or other, nothing from the common fund of mankind's worldwide ideas, unsubordinated to the influence of any general law, indeed isolated from the human family and withdrawn wholly within itself, necessarily undergoes a degradation in proportion to the amount of its own active insubordination. Really, never was any other nation reduced to such a state of humiliation that it became the booty, not for another people, but for some traders who, even though subjects themselves in their own country, became absolute potentates there among them. Moreover, besides this incredible degradation of the Indians, the result of conquest, the actual decay of the Indian society, as we know, dates back even further; this literature, this philosophy, and even the language by which it was all disseminated, belong to an order of things which ceased to exist a long time ago.

again. Since the globe has been circumnavigated by Europe, since a new world, arisen from the ocean, has been made over by Europe, and since the remaining human populations have become so subjugated to her that they exist, as it were, only by Europe's kind permission, it is easy to understand what happened on earth when the old edifice fell and the new arose miraculously in its place: at that time the moral element in the universe received a new law, a new organization. Materials from the ancient world were certainly used in the construction of the new, for supreme reason could not destroy its own handiwork; the material basis of the moral order always remained the same; besides, completely new human stock, drawn from groups unexplored by ancient civilizations, was again furnished by Providence. The energetic, concentrated, northern qualities were combined with the expansive southern and eastern powers; the cold, earnest thought from severe climates fused with the warm, jocular thought from temperate climates. It looked as if all the intellectual powers strewn out across the world came together and mingled on that day, in order to beget whole generations of ideas whose elements had been enshrouded in the most mysterious depths of the human heart up to that time. But neither the plan for the edifice nor the cement which connected the diverse materials was the work of man: it is the idea of truth come down from heaven which accomplished everything. That is what we have to understand and that is the immense fact which a purely historical reasoning process could never clarify in a satisfactory intellectual way through a mere recourse to all the human activities to be found within this epoch. This is the pivot upon which the entire historical sphere turns; this is what explains and proves the whole phenomenon of the education of mankind. The magnificence of the event, its intimate, necessary, wholly providential connection with its antecedents and its consequences would alone be enough, I believe, to place it beyond the ordinary course of human affairs, but the direct effects of this event upon the intellect, the new enriching forces, the new needs created by it, and above all, this general intellectual improvement caused by it, which made man eager for truth and capable of understanding truth in every situation—that is what stamps this historical period completely with an astounding character of providence and supreme reason.

Moreover, notice, even if human reason frequently reverts to things which no longer would, could, or do exist, yet is not human reason basically attached to this moment at all times, no matter what? For the present, is not the whole consciousness of universal intelligence to be found in essence within the new moral order? Does not this portion of universal intelligence, which dominates and carries along the rest of the masses today, really date from the first day of our era? Is not the world spirit the Christian spirit today? I do not know, perhaps everyone cannot see the dividing line which separates us from the ancient world. As for me, all my philosophy, all my ethics, all my religion lies in that concept. There will come a time, I hope, when all the reversions to paganism, such as the one brought about in the fifteenth century, improperly called, I believe, the literary renaissance with all its consequences and results, will be remembered by modern people in the same way that they recall some foolish, guilty, youthful drunkenness which has to be erased from the memory of the world in every possible way.

Note also that by a kind of optical illusion men think of antiquity as a succession of ages with end, whereas the modern world seems to have begun only yesterday. However, the history of the ancient world, for example, as far back as the establishment of the Pelasgians in Greece, takes in a space of time which surpasses the duration of our era by but one century more or less. But the historical time-periods are even shorter than that. During this short space of time how many societies perished in the ancient world! Whereas, in the history of modern people, one simply sees the geographical changes of state boundaries; the society and the people remain intact. I do not have to tell you that such facts as the expulsion of the Moors in Spain, the destruction of the American tribes, and the annihilation of the Tatars in Russia simply help to support the principle. So the fall of the Ottoman empire which already resounds in our ears is again going to offer the spectacle of one of these great catastrophes which Christian people are never going to suffer. Then it will be the turn of other non-Christian people who live at the utmost boundaries of our system. This is the circle of the omnipotent action of sacred truth; in one case by repulsing groups of people, in another case by including them within its circumference, the circle of omnipotent action of sacred truth is enlarged incessantly and brings us near to the time of fulfillment. The destinies of mankind are achieved in this way.

The indifference with which men have treated modern civilization for such a long time is a thing to marvel at. But you see that a proper understanding and perfect explanation of it would be, as it were, the solution to the whole social problem. So, for better or worse, men must go back to this civilization in their most comprehensive, general consideration about the philosophy of history. Really, does it not include the product of all past ages? Will the ages to come be anything else but the result of this civilization? For, moral being is nothing but a product of history and one which history has to complete. Has the fund of worldwide ideas ever existed in so concentrated a manner as in the present Christian society? Has a single thought in the universal history of mankind ever embraced the total activity of man's nature as in our day?

First of all, we are positively the inheritors of all that mankind has ever said or done; there is no place on earth which has escaped the influence of our ideas; indeed, there is actually only one single intellectual force in the whole universe. Thus, all the fundamental questions in the philosophy of history are necessarily contained in the single question of European civilization. But when men disseminate their words about human perfectibility and the progress of the human spirit, they think that they have said and explained everything—as if man has done nothing all the time but progress without ever stopping or going backwards, as if the natural intellectual movement never experienced a standstill or retrogression, nothing but development and progress. But, if this were so, why have these people whom I just mentioned before never budged as long as we have known them? They say that the Asiatic nations are stationary. But why are they stationary? To reach their present-day condition, they apparently must have done what we did—seek, invent, and discover. Then why is it that, once they had reached a certain point, they abruptly halted and have not been able to conceive or create anything new since then?*

The answer is very simple: the progress of human nature is not at all indefinite, as men imagine; there is a limit beyond which it could never pass. That is why the societies of the ancient world have not always advanced, why Egypt, since Herodotus' visit, did not make any progress up to the time of the Greek domination, and why the beautiful, brilliant Roman world which united all the cultures of that time from the columns of Hercules to the Ganges had reached that stage of immobility necessarily terminating all purely human progress at the moment when a new idea came to enlighten the human spirit. If men meditate ever so little upon this fruitful moment without classic prejudices, the scourge of history, they will certainly note that, besides the excessive depravity of morals, the loss of all feeling for virtue, liberty, and love of country,

* When a civilized nation is said to be stationary, it must be clarified when it became that way; otherwise no conclusion can be drawn from this fact.

and besides a genuine decadence in all branches of human knowledge, there was a complete stagnation in everything else. Their minds were incapable of motion except within a narrow, miserable circle through which they broke only in order to precipitate into stupid disorder. Once material interest is satisfied, man no longer advances; he is lucky if he does not go backwards. That is a fact. Do not be mistaken about it, in Greece as in India, in Rome as in Japan, in Mexico as in China all intellectual labor, however prodigious it might have been or may still be, did and still does aim at only one thing. The most exalted and exuberant aspects in the teachings and intellectual habits of the East, far from contradicting this general fact, on the contrary confirm it. For who can fail to note that all these disordered intellectual outbursts originate simply from illusions and delusions about the material nature of man? All that you have to realize is that this earthly interest, an eternal spur for all human activity, is not confined solely to sensual appetites, but that it is quite simply the general need for well-being which manifests itself in all kinds of ways depending upon the level of society and upon various, diverse local causes, but, noneless, it never definitely rises to the level of a purely moral need. The Christian society alone is genuinely animated by interests in thought and in the soul. And that is precisely what constitutes the perfectibility of modern people and that is where the mystery of civilization is to be found. No matter how this other interest occurs there, you will find that it is always subordinated to this powerful force which masters all the faculties in man's soul, places all the powers of reason and feeling at its disposal, and leads everything within man towards the fulfillment of his destiny. This type of interest could assuredly never be satisfied; it is infinite and that is why Christian people must always advance. And, even though the goal aimed at has nothing in common with that finite well-being which is the only one accessible to non-Christian people, yet Christian people find finite well-being also along their route and utilize it; and the joys of life which other people seek exclusively, Christians also gain finally, but through another life according to the words of the Saviour: "Seek ye first the kingdom of God and his justice and all will be added unto you."[11] In this way the enormous development which the dominating spirit communicates to all the intellectual capabilities within these people also showers them with all temporal as well as spiritual goods. Besides, it is certain that a Chinese immobility, a Greek decadence, or even less likely, any total annihilation of civilization will never become part of our experience. Just look around to be convinced of that. The entire globe would have to be overthrown from top to bottom, a second upheaval similar to the one which gave the globe its present form, would have to be repeated, in order to destroy the present civilization. A total destruction of our culture would be inconceivable with anything less than a second cataclysm on a universal scale. And should one of the two hemispheres be totally engulfed, whatever of our civilization would remain in the other would be enough to regenerate the human spirit. Never, no, never will the idea destined to conquer the universe halt or perish. To do that, a specific decree from Him Who put it in the human soul would have to smash it from on high. Finally, Madame, I hope that you will find that this philosophical conclusion derived from meditation upon history is more positive, more evident, and more instructive, if I am right, than all those conclusions peculiarly drawn from the old, banal history[12] taken from the panorama of the centuries by working out the effects of soil, race, and especially the famous theory of human *perfectibility*.

Do you know, Madame, who is responsible for the fact that the influence of Christianity upon society and upon the development of the human spirit is not yet sufficiently understood and appreciated? It is the fault of those who shattered the moral unity; those who date Christianity only from their arrival upon the scene; those who call themselves reformers. It is clear that they are not at all interested in following the march of Christianity throughout the Middle Ages. This entire immense period is simply a void in time for them. Then how could they possibly understand the education of modern people? Believe me, nothing has done more to disfigure the image of modern history than the Protestant point of view. From that comes the exaggerated importance attached to the literary renaissance, a thing which, strictly speaking, never took place, since literature was never wholly lost; that is also why men imagined myriad diverse causes for progress which have basically had only an extremely secondary influence or which simply arise out of the unique cause of everything. That is why men have sought the causes for people's progress everywhere except where they really are and have thus denied Christianity. But, since a less narrow, loftier-minded philosophy has concentrated upon the study of this interesting period through a fortunate return to the past, many new things which were ignored up to now have been suddenly revealed to human thought, so that even the most obstinate ill-will could no longer resist these new factors. If it is in God's providence that men will be enlightened in this fashion, the time is not far off when a great light is going to flash in the obscurity which still covers the history of modern society, and this new philosophy of history, which I want to give you some idea of, is certainly soon going to be understood by men.*

You must admit that this stubbornness on the part of Protestants is strange. In their minds, since the second or third centuries Christianity ceased to exist except for that which was absolutely necessary so as to avoid utter destruction. They look upon the superstition and ignorance of these eleven or twelve centuries in such a way that they see an idolatry there even more deplorable than that of the pagans. In their opinion, if the Waldensians[14] had not come along, the thread of sacred tradition would have been entirely broken, and, if Luther had not come, Christ's religion would have ceased to exist within a few more days. But, please tell me, how can one recognize the divine

---

* Since these lines have been written, M. Guizot has fulfilled our hopes in great part.[13]

seal in this weak, fleeting, lifeless doctrine which they make out of Christianity? How can one see the work of God in this passing, lying doctrine which, instead of regenerating humanity and permeating it with new life, as it promised, has appeared upon earth only in order to pass away, has been born only to die, or simply in order to serve as an instrument for human passions? Did the fate of religion hang then upon Leo X's desire to finish St. Peter's basilica? In their minds if he had not caused indulgences to be sold in Germany for that purpose at that time, there would scarcely be any vestiges of Christianity left in our day. I do not know of anything which would allow you to see the radical vice of the Reformation better than this narrow and niggardly way of considering the revealed religion. Does it not contradict the very words of Jesus Christ, as well as the whole idea of His religion? If His Word is supposed to last longer than sky or earth and He Himself be incessantly among us, then how could the temple which He had erected with His own hands have been upon the brink of collapse? How could this temple have remained empty for such a long time like an abandoned house ready to fall in ruins?

However, one must admit that the Protestants were consequential. They set all of Europe on fire, then cut the bonds uniting Christian people in one single family; they spread so much misery and blood upon earth, because, as they saw it, Christianity was on the point of perishing. Did not everything have to be sacrificed in order to save it? But look at the facts: on the contrary, there is nothing which proves the divinity of our religion better than its perpetual and incessant influence upon the human spirit—an influence which far from ceasing completely has, on the contrary, never slowed down for a moment in its efforts to fit in with the times and to combine with the needs of different peoples and centuries. In this regard reason is satisfied best by this spectacle of its sovereign power which is constantly active amid the infinite obstacles which have not stopped arousing vice within our nature and the fatal, pagan heritage.

Then what is the meaning of the assertion that the Catholic Church had degenerated since the time of the primitive Church? Did not the Church fathers deplore the corruption among Christians after the third century? And were not the same complaints always issued in every century and at every council? Did not true piety always raise its voice against the abuses and vices of the clergy and against encroachments by the hierarchy? There is nothing more admirable than the brilliant illuminations which shot forth from time to time from the depths of the dark night covering the world: sometimes there were examples of the most sublime virtue, at other times there were marvelous effects of the faith upon the spirit of peoples and individuals; the Church gathered all that in and made it part of its strength and richness; thus the eternal edifice was erected in the way which could best provide it with the form needed. Naturally the primitive purity of Christianity could not be preserved for all time; Christianity had to pass through all the phases of corruption and to bear all the characteristics which the freedom of

156

human reason had to imprint upon it. Besides, the perfection of the apostolic church was that of a small community lost in the great pagan community; as a result, the perfection of the apostolic Church could not be that of universal society of mankind. The Golden Age of the Church, we know, was that of its greatest sufferings, the age in which the work of sorrow was operating to found the new order, the age in which the blood of the Saviour still streamed; it is absurd to dream of the return to a state of things which resulted only from the immense miseries which burdened the first Christians.

But do you want to know what caused this reformation which boasts of having rediscovered Christianity? You realize that it is one of the greatest questions which historical science can pose. The Reformation set the world back again into the disunity of paganism; it reestablished great national entities, isolated men's souls and minds, plunged man again into the solitude of passion, and tried to remove all the mutual understanding and harmony which the Saviour brought into the world. The Reformation may have accelerated the movement of the human spirit, but from the consciousness of intelligent being it also removed the fertile, sublime idea of universality and unity, the unique source for the true progress of mankind, i.e., infinite progress. The real effect of every schism within the Christian world is the rupture of this mysterious unity which contains the whole divine idea of Christianity and all its power. For that reason the ancient or primitive Church within which Christianity matured will never compromise with the new, separated sects. Too bad for the Church and for the world, if the fact of the schism is ever recognized by the legitimate authority! All would soon return to a chaos of human ideas, multiplicity of lies, ruin, and dust. The visible, palpable stability of truth is alone capable of preserving the reign of the spirit upon earth. The empire of thought acquires permanence and continuity only by working itself out in the given forms of human nature. And then, what would become of the sacrament of communion, this marvelous discovery of Christian reason which, as it were, materializes souls in order to unify them better, should men no longer desire a visible union and should they be content with an inner community of convictions without any external reality! What good is it to unite with the Saviour, if we are separated from one another? I am not surprised that ferocious Calvin, the assassin of Servetus,[15] the bully Zwingli,[16] and the tyrant Henry VIII with his hypocrite Cranmer[17] misunderstood the powers of love and union contained in the great sacrament; however, what I cannot understand is that profound, genuinely religious spirits often found among the Lutherans who are, moreover, not dogmatic about this despoilation of the Eucharist which their founder combatted with such ardor, could be so strangely mistaken about the nature of this great institution and that they could abandon themselves to deplorable Calvinist teaching. You must agree that there is a strange taste for ruination among the Protestant churches. It could be said that they yearn only for their own annihilation, that they seem to fear becoming too full of life, and that they refuse anything which could make them last too long. Is this then the teaching of Him who came to bring life on earth and who conquered death? Or are we already in heaven, so that we can reject the conditions of earthly order with impunity? And is this order anything but the combination of the pure thoughts on the part of the intelligent being with the things necessary for their existence? But, the first of these necessities is society, the contact of minds, the fusion of ideas and feelings. It is only by finding a satisfactory solution within society that truth comes alive, descends from the region of speculation to that of reality, moves from thought to *fact*, and finally secures the character of a natural force so that its effect becomes as certain as that of every natural force. But how could all that occur in an ideal society which would exist only in man's desires and imagination? That is what the Protestant church is: *invisible just like nothingness.*

The day on which all the Christian sects will reunite will be the one on which the schismatic churches penitently and humbly decide to acknowledge, in sack and cinders, that by separating themselves from the mother Church they rejected the effects of this sublime prayer of the Saviour: Holy Father preserve in thy name those whom thou hast given me, so that they may be one as we are one.[18] Were the papacy, as they suggest, a human institution—as if things of this stature could be made by human hands—what difference would it make? It is certain that in this time the papacy resulted essentially from the spirit of Christianity and that today as a constant visible sign of unity, it is an even greater sign of reunion. On these grounds why not confer precedence over all Christian society upon it? Besides, who will not admire its unique destinies? Despite all its vicissitudes, all its disasters, its own faults and sins, all the attacks of nonbelievers, and even despite the incredible triumph of nonbelief, there it stands firmer than ever! Stripped of its human pomp, the papacy has become stronger, and its continued duration is particularly strengthened and guaranteed by human indifference towards it. In times past it was the veneration on the part of the Christian world which gave the papacy its permanence, a certain instinct in the nations which allowed them to see the cause of their temporal and eternal salvation within it; now it is the papacy's humble attitude amid the powers on earth. But the papacy always perfectly fulfills its aim; it *centralizes* Christian thoughts today, attracts them to one another, reminds even those who have disavowed the unity of the supreme principle of their faith, and always majestically towers above the world of material interests by means of this characteristic divine vocation totally imprinted upon it. No matter how little men seem to be concerned with the papacy now, just let it disappear suddenly from earth by some impossible quirk—then you would see all these religious sects fall into a frenzy, were this living monument in the history of the great community to cease to stand before them. Everywhere men would seek to recover this visible unity which they now treat so lightly, but nowhere would it be found. And, certainly,

Christian reason would lose the present, valuable, full inner awareness of its future which makes Christian reason different from ordinary reason, just as men lose these hopes founded upon the recollection of an active life at the moment when they discover that all this activity is fruitless and that henceforth the very recollection of our past escapes from our memories.

Good day, Madame. I promise you that this time you will not have to wait for the next letter.

LETTER VII

Madame,

The more you think over what I told you the other day, the more you will find that all this has been said already many times by people of all parties and opinions, and that we are only attaching a significance to it which had not been given to it before. Yet I have no doubt that if by some chance these letters were to see the light of day, there would be no shortage of complaints that they are paradoxical. If you uphold, with a certain degree of conviction, even the most ancient ideas, you will invariably find that they will be taken for singular innovations. But I believe that the age of paradox and of systems without basis in reality is so far gone that now one would have to be stupid to fall into the old errors of the human mind. It is certain that if today human reason is not as broad, elevated, or fertile as it was in the grand centuries of inspiration and invention, it is infinitely more strict, more sober, more rigorous, more methodical, in a word, more precise than it ever was; and I shall add with a sense

162

of genuine satisfaction, that for some time it has also become more impersonal than ever, a fact which is the best guarantee against the boldness of individual opinions.

If in our meditations upon man's recollections we have had a few insights of our own which are not in agreement with some preconceptions, that is because we thought that it was time for each man to state his position frankly about these matters, just as men did in the past century with reference to the natural sciences. We believed that it was time to conceive of history in all its rational ideality, just as men have conceived of the natural sciences in all their empirical reality. Since the subject of history and the methods of studying it are always the same, it is evident that the circle of historical experience must be closed one day. The applications will never end but, once the rule is found, there will be nothing to add to it. In the physical sciences each new discovery opens up a new area of study and a new field of observation: as a recent example, has not the microscope alone revealed an entire world unknown to the ancient natural scientists? Thus, progress in the natural sciences is necessarily infinite, but in history it is always man whom we study and always the same instrument which we use in this study. So, if there is a great lesson hidden in history, then men must one day necessarily come to a specific conclusion which will mark the end of experience once and for all. I believe that I cited this beautiful thought of Pascal for you once: that the whole succession of men is nothing but one man who always subsists;[1] well, this

163

thought must one day cease to be the imaginative enunciation of an abstract principle and become the real fact behind human reason which will henceforth be, so to say, forced in each of its acts to set in motion the entire immense chain of human ideas extending across the centuries.

But the following question is asked: Could man ever allow the extremely personal, individual consciousness now found within himself to be supplanted by this general consciousness which would make him constantly feel himself to be part of the great moral totality? Yes, without a doubt. Men must realize that besides the feeling of our personal individuality we also cherish a feeling of our relationship to the fatherland, the family, and the community of opinion to which we belong. This latter feeling is often even stronger than the former. Men must also notice that the germ of a superior consciousness resides within us in a very genuine way and forms the essence of our nature, and that the present *ego* is not imposed upon us by an inevitable law but has been created by ourselves. Then men will see that man's whole aim on earth consists in annihilating his personal existence and substituting a completely social or impersonal one for it. You have seen that this is the unique basis for moral philosophy.* You now realize that it is also the basis for the idea of history. From this point of view all the illusions which cover or disfigure the different ages in the general life of mankind could be treated

* See the second letter.

not with cold, scientific interest but with the deep sense of moral truth. How can man identify himself with something which has never taken place? How can he become linked *with nothingness?* Both types of attracting forces occur in the truth alone. In the study of history we should become used to never compromising with the daydreams of the imagination or with the habits of recollection, but rather let us be as ardent in the search for positive knowledge and certitude as men have always been when in pursuit of the picturesque and the amusing. There is no point in filling our memories with more facts; there are too many facts in man's memory now. It is erroneous to imagine that the mass of factual data necessarily results in certitude. In general, the lack of factual material does not cause historical hypothesizing, nor does factual ignorance cause historical ignorance; it is rather the lack of historical reflection and reasoning. If men should seek to obtain certitude and to reach some positive knowledge in this scientific field simply upon the basis of facts, is it not apparent that there will never be enough of them? Oftentimes a single trait which is properly grasped clarifies and proves better than a whole chronicle. Here then is our rule: let us meditate upon the facts which we know about and try to have living images rather than dead matter in our minds. Let others tire themselves by rummaging around in the old dust of history as much as they want, as for us, we have other things to do. Thus, we consider historical data as perfectly complete but have little confidence in historical logic (we are always cautious about that and always have to scrutinize it carefully). If, like others, we find nothing but human reason and some perfectly free wills within the stream of history, then we will not find what we are looking for in history, even though we may vainly try to cram our minds with facts and arrange them most marvelously in causal relationships. In such a case, we would always simply see the same human game which everyone has seen there in every historical period.* And it would always be this dynamic, psychological history, which I told you about earlier, which attempts to make everything reasonable through the individual, through an imaginary chain of causes and effects, through men's imaginations and the supposedly inevitable consequences of these flights of imagination, and which also hands human intelligence over to its own law. This shows a lack of understanding for the fact that the influence of a supreme law must necessarily be all the more evident there, due to the infinite superiority of this part of our complete nature over the other.**

* One cannot reproach Herodotus, Titus-Livy, or Gregory of Tours for not having had Providence intervene in human affairs; however, must we point out that we are not advocating that the human spirit return to the concept of his superstitious daily intervention of God?
** In this Rome, which people talk so much about, which everybody visits but understands so little, there is a unique monument which can be termed an ancient reality which still endures, an event from another age which has paused in our times: I refer to the Colosseum. In my opinion, there is no factor in history which suggests such profound ideas as the sight of these ruins, which makes the character of two of mankind's ages stand out, and which proves so well this great

And here is one of the most remarkable examples of the duplicity in certain popular concepts of history as it is presented today: you know that the Greeks make art a comprehensive idea of the human spirit. Look at what constitutes this magnificent creation of Hellenic genius. The material side of man was idealized, heightened, apotheosized; the natural, legitimate order of things was reversed; what should have remained forever in the lower regions of the intellectual world was

historical axiom, namely, that there was never any real progress or genuine stability in society before the Christian epoch. This is the arena where the Roman people assembled to steep themselves in blood, where the whole pagan world was epitomized so well in a terrible game, and where the whole life of these times was displayed with its most lively pleasures and most dazzling pomp. Does it not stand there before us in order to tell us what the world had come to when all the forces within human nature had been used up in the construction of the social edifice, when its fall was already evident all over, and when a new era of barbarism was going to start once again? There too for the first time the blood was spilled which was going to moisten the foundations of the new edifice. So, does this monument all by itself not deserve a complete book? It it strange that the Colosseum has never inspired an historical thought full of great truths! Among the swarms of travelers who flocked to Rome there was one who went to a very famous, neighboring height from which he could calmly contemplate the Colosseum in its astounding setting and he thought he saw the centuries roll along before his eyes and teach him the enigma behind their movement, he claimed. Well, this man really only saw the victors and the Capuchins! As if the only things which happened there were triumphs and processions! A petty, trivial idea which gave birth to the deceitful production[2] which everybody knows: a real prostitution of one of the most beautiful, historical spirits which ever existed!

placed on a level with man's loftiest thoughts. The influence of the senses upon man's spirit was augmented infinitely; the great line of demarcation which separates the divine and the human within man's perception was broken. This resulted in chaotic confusion of all moral components. The intellect pounced upon things which were the least worthy of its attention, as if these were the important things to know; an incredible allure was imparted to the most vicious aspects of human nature; a sensuous and deceitful poetry was introduced into the imagination in place of the intellectual, truthful primitive poetry, and this powerful faculty, created in order for us to represent the unrepresentable and to see the unseeable, was henceforth employed only to render the sensuous even more sensuous, the earthy even more earthy; the result was that our physical being grew while our moral being was shrunk. And, though some wise men, such as Pythagoras and Plato, fought against this fatal tendency of the spirit of their times, they themselves were more or less invaded by this spirit; their efforts accomplished nothing, and it is only after Christianity had regenerated the human spirit that their teachings acquired genuine influence. That is what Greek art did. It is the apotheosis of matter, no one can deny. Well, have people understood it in this way? No, far from it. People look at the remaining monuments of this art, without understanding what they mean; men take delight in viewing these admirable inspirations of a spirit which fortunately no longer exists, but men do not even suspect what happens in the impure heart and the deceitful spirit. It is a cult, a drunkenness, a fascination which rots our sense of morality. However, when in the state of this imbecilic admiration, man need only exercise his cool reasoning-power upon what he feels, in order to recognize that it comes from the vilest part of our being, because, to coin a phrase, it is with our bodies that we understand these bodies made of marble and bronze. And notice that all the beauty and all the perfection of these figures simply comes from the perfect stupidity which they express; but just let a sign of reason dare to appear in their traits and the ideal which charms us would disappear immediately. Thus, this is not even the representation of a reasonable being which we contemplate but some kind of human animal, a fictitious being, a kind of monster produced by the most disordered excesses of the human spirit, and its image should not only not give us any pleasure but should really be repulsive to us. This is how the gravest questions in the philosophy of history are disfigured and obscured by prejudice, these habits from school, these intellectual routines, and this charm of a deceiving illusion which form the present-day idea of history.

Perhaps you will ask me if I myself have always been a stranger to these seductions of art? No, Madame, on the contrary; some sort of instinct had revealed them to me as sweet enchantments which ought to fill my life, long before I actually knew them. When one of the great events of the century brought me to the capital in which conquest had momentarily assembled so many marvels, I did as the others and acted even more devoutly, I offered my incense upon the altar of the idols.[3] Later when I had seen them for a second time[4] in the light of their native sun, I again took great delight in them. But it is also true that something bitter, similar to remorse, was always hiding at the bottom of this delight; moreover, when I realized the truth, I did not avoid any of its consequences but rather accepted all of them at once without evasion.

But, Madame, let us return to these great historical personalities whom I referred to the other day as misunderstood or misplaced by history. Without that you would have an incomplete idea of this matter. Let us begin with Moses, the most gigantic and imposing of all historical figures.

Thank God, we no longer live at the time when the great Jewish legislator was considered simply to be one of those creatures belonging to the world of fiction—even for those who bothered to study him earnestly; he was like all these supernatural heroes, demigods, and prophets which one finds upon the first pages of the histories of ancient people or a poetic personality studied by history simply from the viewpoint of its instructive value as a type, symbol or expression of the era in which he is placed according to human tradition. Nobody today can doubt, I think, the historical reality of Moses. Nevertheless, there is no doubt that the sacred atmosphere encircling him is not good for him and that it has prevented him from occupying the place which belongs to him in history. This great man's influence upon humanity is not as well understood and appreciated as it should be. His features remain too veiled in the mysterious light covering them. Since he has not been studied enough, Moses does not provide the lessons usually resulting from the appearance of great men in history. Neither public figure nor private individual, neither thinker nor man of action discovers all the teaching that could be found in the story of Moses' life. This results from habits ushered into the mind by religion in impressing a superhuman appearance upon the biblical figures and making them appear completely different from what they really are.* One cannot meditate enough upon Moses' personality, a curious mixture of eminence and simplicity, forcefulness and kindheartedness, hardness and sweetness. There is, I believe, no single character which offers a combination of such opposite traits and talents. And when I think about this prodigious creature and about the effects which he had upon men I do not know what I should admire more: the historic phenomenon which he caused or the moral phenomenon which I find in him as a person.

On the one hand, there is this immense conception

---

* Note that basically biblical personalities should be those best known to us, for there are no others whose traits are traced better. This is one of the strong points in Scripture. Since people were supposed to be able to identify themselves with these men who were supposed to act directly upon our most intimate feelings, in order to prepare our souls in this way to submit to the otherwise necessary influence of Christ's person, the Scriptures discovered the secret of drawing their traits so well that their images are engraved upon man's mind, so as to create the impression of men whom one has known intimately.

of a chosen people, i.e., a people armed with the supreme mission of guarding the idea of one God on earth and this spectacle of the extraordinary means which he utilized to organize this people in such a way that they would preserve this idea, not only intact but so that one day the idea could appear powerful and irresistible, like a natural force outshining all human powers and bringing the whole intellectual world into submission. On the other hand, there is the man whose simplicity was almost a weakness, capable of giving vent to his wrath merely in an ineffectual manner, able to command only by wearing himself out in argumentation; he accepts the advice of the first man who comes along: a strange genius, the strongest and most docile of men at one and the same time! He engenders the times to come and humbly submits to all that is offered to him under the guise of truth; he speaks to men from the midst of a meteor, his voice resounds throughout the centuries, he strikes people like destiny and yet gives in to the first sign of a sensitive heart and to the first just reason which accosts him! Is there not a surprising greatness, a unique lesson in that?

Men have tried to diminish this greatness by stating that at first he had only dreamed of delivering his people from an unbearable yoke, although men honor him for the heroism he displayed in his work. Men have pretended to see him only as a great legislator and today, I believe, they discover an admirable liberalism in his laws. It has also been said that his God was simply a national God and that he had taken over all his theosophy from the Egyptians. He was certainly

a patriot but what great soul is not, no matter what his
mission on earth may be? Besides, there is a general
law: one must work within the domestic circle in
which one is placed and have an effect upon one's
natural, social family, in order to have an effect upon
men; one must address oneself to one's nation, in order
to speak distinctly to mankind, otherwise one will not
be heard, and nothing will be accomplished. The more
direct and practical man's moral action upon his neigh-
bors is, the more definite and strong it is; the more
personal the expression, the more powerful it is. Nothing helps us towards a better understanding of *the
supreme principle* behind the actions of this man than
the perfect efficacy and justice of the means he utilized, in order to achieve the work which he had in
mind. It is possible that he had found the idea of a
national God among his own or among other people
and that he had made use of this given reality, like so
many others which he found in his natural predeces-
sors, in order to introduce his sublime monotheism into
human thought. But it does not follow from this that
Jehovah was not the God of the whole earth for him
as He is for Christians. The more he sought to isolate
and reinforce this great dogma in his nation, the more
he employed extraordinary means in order to attain
this end, and the more throughout all this work by a
superior reason one can discern the wholly universal
thought of preserving the notion of the unique God for
the entire world and all for all generations to come. In
the construction of an inviolable sanctuary to the true
God amid the polytheism pervading the whole earth

at that time was there any surer method than by inspiring the people, guardian of the sacred monument, with a racial abhorrence for all idolatrous people and by binding the entire social existence of this people, their whole destiny, memory, and hope to this single principle? Read Deuteronomy with this in mind and you will be surprised how much light it throws upon Moses' system, as well as upon the whole philosophy of revelation.

Each word in this unusual book reveals the *superhuman* idea which dominated the spirit of its author. This also explains these frightening exterminations ordained by Moses, which are in such strange contrast with the sweetness of his nature and which disgusted a philosophy even more foolish than impious.[5] This philosophy did not comprehend that the man who was such a prodigious instrument in the hands of Providence and the one entrusted with its secrets could only act as Providence and nature. The times and generations could not have any sort of value for him; his mission was not directed at offering a model of justice and moral perfection but at giving the human spirit an immense idea which the human spirit *could not have produced by itself.* Do you believe that he was only dreaming of colonizing the stupid and unmanageable rabble which he was leading, when he repressed the cry of his affectionate heart, as he commanded the massacre of nations and as he lowered the sword of divine justice upon whole groups of people? What a brilliant psychology! What will it not do to avoid the real cause of the phenomenon under consideration? It relieves itself of any trouble by combining the most contradictory traits within the same soul, though no one has ever experienced such a combination in any single individual!

And does it matter, after all, if Moses borrowed some teachings from Egyptian wisdom? Does it matter if he had at first simply thought of freeing his nation from the yoke of servitude? If he embodied in his people the thought which he picked up somewhere or drew from the depths of his soul, surrounded it with all the elements of preservation and continuity in human nature, and in this way gave the true God to man, so that the entire intellectual development resulting from this principle is due incontestably to him, would it be any less true because of that?

David is one of the historical personages whose characteristics have been passed on to us very well. There is nothing as lively, dramatic, and true as his history, nothing as marked as his features. The account of his life, his sublime songs in which the present disappears so admirably into the future, portray the interior of his soul so well that there is absolutely nothing in his existence which is hidden from us. Nevertheless, he makes an impression like the Greek or Roman heroes upon profoundly religious spirits. Once again, the trouble is that all these great men in the Bible belong to another world; the halo glowing over their heads unfortunately relegates them to a region where the mind does not like to travel, a region of importunate forces commanding inflexible submission, where men exist perpetually in the presence of implacable law, and where the only thing to do is kneel down and adore. However, how can one understand historical movement if one does not study it there where the principle creating the movement manifests itself best?

In contrasting Socrates and Marcus Aurelius with these two giants in Scripture, I wanted to make you judge the two worlds from which they are drawn, through this contrast of such different forms of greatness. Read the anecdotes about Socrates in Xenophon first without the presumptions attached to his name, if you can; think over how much his death added to his renown; think about his famous demon and this complacency with vice which he pushed to an unusual degree, you must admit;* mull over the different accusations with which his contemporaries charged him; think over the words which he pronounced just before his death and which bequeathed all the incertitude of his thought to posterity; finally think about all the divergent, absurd, contradictory opinions which issued from his school: As for Marcus Aurelius, let us get rid of the superstition about him too; meditate properly on his book; remember the massacre at Lyons, the appalling fellow to whom he delivered the universe, the times in which he lived, the high society in which he was placed, and finally all the means of greatness offered by his position in the world. Then please compare the result of Socratic philosophy with

* If I were not writing to a woman, I would have suggested that the reader read Plato's *Symposium* to get an idea of what I mean.

176

that of Mosaic religion, the personage of the Roman emperor with that of the man who, though a herdsman, became king, poet, sage and thus personified the vast, mysterious conception of the prophetic legislator and was made the focal point in this marvelous world in which the goals of humanity were destined for fulfillment. He is the one who definitively determined his people's inclination which was specifically and profoundly religious, and in this way he created the earthly order of things which was alone capable of rendering the generation of truth possible here below. Undoubtedly you agree then that if poetical thought represents men such as Moses and David like superhuman beings and surrounds them with an extraordinary brilliance, universal reason should also be objectively prone to see within them something more than simply the great, extraordinary life of the universe; these men were certainly completely direct manifestations of the supreme law governing the universe, and their appearance can be compared to these great epochs in the physical order which change or regenerate nature from time to time.*

Epicurus comes next. You believe that I do not attach any particular importance to the reputation of this personage. But first of all, you have to realize that

* Nevertheless, there is nothing simpler than the enormous glory of Socrates, the only man from the ancient world who died for a conviction. This unique example of heroic faith must have really staggered these people. But is it not silly for us to be as mistaken about Socrates as they were, since it is we who have seen whole populations give up their lives for the cause of truth?

177

his materialism did not differ in any way from the ideas of the other ancient philosophers; however, since Epicurus had a more frank and more coherent critical sense than most of them he did not become entangled in endless contradictions as they did. Pagan deism appeared to him what it really was, namely, an absurdity, its spiritualization a deception. His physics which was nothing more than that of Democritus, whom Bacon called somewhere the only reasonable physicist among the ancients, was not inferior to that of the other natural scientists in his day and as for his atomic theory, if you discard the metaphysics from it, it is not as ridiculous as men have said, since the molecular theory has become such a positive thing in our day. But, as you know, his name is principally linked up with his ethics, and that is the reason for his bad reputation. But we judge this morality only on the basis of his sect's licentiousness and upon more or less arbitrary interpretations made by men after his death; his own writings, as you know, have not come down to us. It is undoubtedly all right for Cicero to fear voluptuousness at the very mention of his name; however, just look at this discredited morality, study it correctly and principally with reference to what we know about the author's own personal life, and disregard what results it had in the pagan world, since the result belongs much more to the general attitude of the human spirit in these times than to the teachings of Epicurus. Then compare this teaching with the other moral systems of antiquity and you will find it not as arrogant, hard, and impractical as that of the Stoics nor as vague, nebu-

lous, and powerless as that of the Platonists. This moral doctrine was kindly, benevolent, and human, so that in a way it contained something of the principle in Christian morality. There is no way of misunderstanding the fact that this philosophy contained an essential element which was totally lacking in the practical thought of antiquity, an element of unity, solidarity, and goodwill among men. This philosophy had common sense and an absence of pride in a special way which is not to be found in contemporary philosophies. Besides, this philosophy had the sovereign good consist in peace of soul and sweet joy imitating the heavenly goodness of the gods upon earth. Epicurus himself provided a good example of this peaceable existence; he lived almost obscurely in the bosom of sweet friendship and study. If his morality could have been inculcated into the spirit of people without allowing itself to become perverted by the vicious principle dominating the world then, I am sure that his morality would have filled men's hearts with a sweetness and a humanity which the boastful morality of the Stoics and the dreamy speculation of the Academicians would have been incapable of inculcating. Please note then that Epicurus is the only wise man in antiquity who led a perfectly irreproachable moral life and the only one whose disciples remembered him with feelings of love and veneration which were like a cult.*
Now you understand why we have had to rectify our ideas about this a little.

* Pythagoras is no exception. He was a fictitious personage to whom men ascribed whatever they wanted.

179

We shall not go back to Aristotle. He does form one of the most important chapters in modern history, but this is too large a subject to be simply treated in a superficial manner. Only please notice that Aristotle is in a certain sense a creation of the new spirit. It is natural that in its youth modern reason, tormented by its enormous need to know, became wholly attached to this intellectual mechanic who made understanding move forward with a prodigious velocity through the use of his cranks, levers, and pulleys. And it was also very understandable that the Arabs, who unearthed him first, should have found him so much to their tastes. This impoverished people had nothing of its own which evoked any kind of attachment; so naturally a wholly completed wisdom appealed to them. At last all that has passed away: Arabs, Scholastics, and their common master, they have all fulfilled their different missions. All that has restored more consistency, more aplomb to the mind; its activity has become more assured and that has produced a method of procedure which facilitates the movements and accelerates the operations of the mind. Everything has turned out for the best, as you notice; evil has turned into good thanks to the power and hidden enlightenment in modern reason. Today we have to retrace our steps and retravel the wide roads of days gone by when our intellect had no machines at its disposal other than golden-blue wings of its angelic nature.

Let us turn to Mohammed. Think about the good which his religion did for humanity: first, because it contributed to the destruction of polytheism along with other more powerful causes, also because it disseminated the idea of one God and one universal faith in an immense territory of the globe and even into regions which could be termed inaccessible to the general intellectual movement. Thus, Mohammed's religion prepared innumerable groups of people for the definitive destiny of mankind. Men could not fail to recognize that, despite the debt which this great man owed to his time and his birthplace, he merits men's respect infinitely more than this mob of useless wise men who were incapable of ever giving body and life to any of their ideas, or of filling a simple heart with a strong conviction, and who have had only a divisive influence upon human nature, instead of trying to unify the scattered elements in man's nature. Islamism is one of the most remarkable manifestations of a general law: any other kind of judgment reveals a misunderstanding of Christianity's universal influence, the source of Islam. The most essential quality of our religion is its power to assume the most diversified forms of religious thought and to know how to become linked, when necessary, even with error, in order to achieve its total result. *Mohammed's religion should be considered one of the branches in the great historical development of the revealed religion.* The most intolerant dogmatists should have no difficulty admitting this important fact and they would certainly do so, should they once become aware of what makes us regard the Mohammedans as our natural enemies, for our prejudice arises solely from that thing.* Besides, you know that practically every chapter in the Koran makes reference to Jesus Christ. But we agree that men have no clear idea about the great work of redemption and no understanding of the mystery of Christ's reign, so long as they do not see the influence of Christianity in every place where just the name of the Saviour is pronounced and as long as men do not perceive that it exercises an influence upon every spirit who somehow comes in contact with His teaching. Otherwise we would have to exclude entire multitudes who call themselves Christians from the benefits of redemption. But would this not result in reducing the kingdom of Jesus Christ to a very minor thing and the university of Christianity to a ridiculous fiction?

Thus, since Mohammedanism is a result of the religious fermentation introduced in the East by the appearance of the new religion, it occupies one of first places in the list of things which do not at first seem to originate from Christianity but which certainly do come from it. As a result, besides the negative effect which Mohammedanism had upon the formation of Christian society by fusing the particular interests of people into that of the common good, besides the numerous materials that Arabic civilization furnished our own—things which must be considered as the

* In the beginning the Mohammedans had no antipathy towards Christians; their hatred and disdain for Christianity initially came as the result of long wars with the Christians. It was natural for Christians to consider them first idolaters and then as enemies of their religion, which the Mohammedans eventually became in reality.

indirect ways utilized by Providence, in order to consumate the regeneration of humanity—in Islam's own influence upon the spirit of people submitted to it we have to recognize a direct and positive effect of the doctrine from which it is derived and which has simply adjusted itself there to certain demands of time and place, in order to achieve the means of spreading the seed of truth upon an even vaster territory. There is no doubt that those who serve the Lord with knowledge and conviction are fortunate! But let us not forget that in the world there is an infinite number of forces obeying the voice of Christ without having any notion of the supreme power which sets them in motion!

Homer is our last subject for discussion. The question of Homer's influence upon the human spirit has been completely settled in our time. Today we know what Homeric poetry really is and how it contributed to the formation of the Greek character which, in turn, determined that of the entire ancient world. We know that this poetry replaced another loftier, purer poetry of which only fragments remain. We also know that Homeric poetry substituted a new order of ideas in place of the old order of ideas which did not originate on Grecian soil and that these primitive ideas, pushed into the background by the new thought, found refuge either in the mysteries of Samothrace or else in the shade of other sanctuaries dedicated to lost truths, and that from that time onwards only a small number of elect or initiates knew of their existence.* Men do not

---

* If you want to get an idea of Homer's moral influence in the world, simply read Plutarch's study or the chapter

realize, I find, how Homeric elements still to be found within the consciousness of mankind can have something in common with the times in which we live. Now that is precisely what interests the real philosophy of history, since its principal study, as you have seen, consists simply in the search for the permanent results and eternal effects of historical phenomena.

Thus, in our opinion, Homer is still simply the Typhon[8] or the Ahriman[9] of the present world, as he was in this world which he created. As we see it, deadly heroism based on passion, impetuous ideal of beauty, and unbridled taste for the earth all comes to us from him.* Note that there was nothing like that in the other civilized societies of the world. The Greeks were the only ones who dared to idealize and divinize vice and crime; they and the people who inherited their civilization were the only ones to develop harmful poetry. In the Middle Ages one can see clearly in what direction the mind of the Christian nations would have developed, if it had completely surrendered to the hand guiding it. This poetry could not possibly

by Maxim of Tyr which deals with Homer. Then read the chapters which deal with Greek civilization in Heeren's book[6] and especially everything relating to this subject in Kreutzer's excellent work.[7]

* The effects of Homeric poetry are naturally connected with those of Greek art, because Homeric poetry is its model; in other words, Homeric poetry formed Greek art and Greek art continued to exercise its effects. It does not matter whether a man such as Homer existed or not, historical criticism will never be capable of annihilating the memory of Homer; so the philosopher should study the idea connected with this memory and not the poet himself.

have come to us from our northern ancestors; the spirit
of northern men was formed in a wholly different manner and aimed at anything but attachment to the earth;
if the spirit of northern men had combined all alone
with Christianity, instead of what happened, it would
have certainly become lost in the nebulous vagueness
of their dreamy fancies. Moreover, we no longer have
any of the blood which flowed in their veins, and it is
not among the people described by Caesar and Tacitus
that we look for lessons on life but rather among
those people in Homer's world.

Only a short time ago a reversion to our own past
started to lead us back to the bosom of our family and
made us rediscover our paternal heritage little by little.
Like northern people, we have inherited only customs
and traditions; the spirit is sustained only by knowledge; the most inveterate customs become lost and the
most enrooted traditions obliterated, when they are
not linked with knowledge. Now, aside from our religious ideas, all our ideas come from the Greeks and
Romans.

So, as for Homeric poetry, after it had led astray the
old western stream of thought which linked men with
the great days of creation, it did the same thing in the
new western world. In coming to us with the science,
philosophy, and literature of the ancients, Homeric
poetry identified us with all that so well that we are
still suspended between the false world and the true
one in the present state of our existence. Even though
men may not concern themselves with Homer today,
and though they certainly do not read his works, none-

theless, his gods and heroes still strongly dispute with the Christian idea for every inch of ground. For there is really an astounding seduction in this wholly earthy and material poetry, so prodigiously sweet to our natural vices, since this poetry weakens the fiber of our reason, holds reason stupidly enchained by its phantoms and its delusions, and rocks reason to sleep with powerful illusions. But, the old, evil impressions will continue to form the most vital, the most active element in our reason, so long as a deep moral sense, derived from a clear view of antiquity and from a complete absorption of the spirit in Christian truth, has not filled our hearts with scorn and disgust for these ages of deception and folly, genuine saturnalia in the life of humanity, which still infatuate us, and so long as some kind of conscious repentance has not made us blush at the mad worship which we have lavished upon these detestable grandeurs for too long a time. As for me, I believe that in order to regenerate ourselves completely in accordance with revealed reason, we still need *some immense penance, some dreadful expiation* decidedly felt by the universal Christian community and generally suffered like a great physical catastrophe on the whole surface of our world; without it I cannot conceive how we could rid ourselves of the mire which still stains our recollections.* That is

* We are really fortunate in our day that the new region just uncovered a while ago for historical consideration was not infected by Homerism. The influence of Indian ideas has made itself felt in a useful way for the advance of philosophy. God grant that by this indirect route we may achieve as soon as possible the goal towards which a shorter route has not been able to lead us up to now!

the way that the philosophy of history should understand Homerism. Therefore, decide for yourself how the philosophy of history should consider Homer. See, if after all that, it is not bound in conscience to affix the seal of an indelible brand upon Homer's forehead. Here we are, Madame at the end of our gallery. I have not told you everything that I wanted to; however, I have to end. But do you know one thing? Basically we Russians have nothing in common with Homer, the Greeks, the Romans, the Germans, and all that. All that is completely foreign to us. But what do you want to do about it? We have to speak the language of Europe. Our exotic civilization has its back turned towards Europe in such a way that, although we do not have its ideas, we have no other language than Europe's own; so, we are thus forced to speak that language. Even if the small number of intellectual habits, traditions, and historical memories which we possess do not bind us to any people upon earth, even if we do not really belong to any of the systems in the moral universe, nonetheless through our social superficialities we tend towards the western world. Without uniting us as intimately to Europe as people imagine and without letting us experience the great movement at work there with our whole being, yet this link, however weak, still makes our future destiny dependent upon that of European society. Therefore, the more we try to identify ourselves with European society, the better off we shall be. Up to now we have lived all alone; what we have learned from others was upon the surface of our being, like a simple decoration, without permeating into the interior of our souls; *today the forces of the sovereign society have grown so much, its work upon the rest of humanity has increased so greatly, that soon we shall be swept along body and soul in the universal whirlwind, that is certain: we surely could not remain in our desert any longer. So let us do all that we can to prepare the way for our descendants.* Since we are not able to leave them what we have not had, such as beliefs, a reasoning-process formed by history, a strongly delineated personality, animated, active, fruitful convictions developed in the course of a long intellectual life, then at least let us leave them a few ideas which, although we ourselves have not found them transmitted from one generation to another, will nonetheless have a certain traditional element and for that reason finally some power and fertility greater than our own thoughts. In this way we shall have merited much for posterity and shall not have lived uselessly upon earth.

Good day, Madame, it will now be solely up to you to make me take up this matter again whenever you want. After all, what is the use of elaborating and exhausting each idea in an intimate conversation full of understanding on both sides? If what I have said to you is enough to cause you to discover some new lesson in the study of history, some interest which is deeper than what is ordinarily found in it, then I am satisfied.

Moscow February 16, 1829

LETTER VIII

Yes, Madame, the time has come to speak the language of simple reason. There is no point any more in having blind faith, beliefs from the heart; we must appeal directly to thought. Sentiment can no longer be discerned through this mass of artificial needs, violent interests, and agonizing preoccupations which invade our lives. In France and in England existence has become too complicated, too prone to particular interests, too individual; in Germany it is too abstract, too peculiar for even the powers of the heart to produce their legitimate effect there. For the moment the rest of the world does not count. Today we must try if possible to reduce everything to a single problem of probabilities, with a solution within the capacities of all intellectuals, which would fit every temperament, not harm anybody's present interests, and thus be able to attract even the most rebellious minds.

This does not mean that feelings are to be forever banished from the intellectual world. God save us, their turn will come again. Then they will reappear stronger, larger, purer than ever. I am certain that this moment is coming soon. But, in our day, in the present situation, feelings are not able to move souls. It is very important to realize this fully. Though some awakening of the lively qualities of mankind's youth is noticeable at this moment, yet this is only the dawn of a beautiful day; the country is still completely covered with the shadows of twilight; only certain peaks begin to catch fire in the first rays of daybreak.

The material proofs of the truth are complete for those who are concerned about it. Do you know, Madame, what I mean by the material proofs of truth? I mean the mass of historical facts which have been properly analyzed. At this time they must be brought together in a systematic and popular form, and they must be expressed in such a way that they may make an impression upon those minds most indifferent to good, those who are the least open to truth, or those who still flounder around in past times, in those times which are all over for everyone else and will, of course, never return, but which still exist for slow hearts and for languid souls who never understand the present day but continue to exist in yesterdays.

This conclusive demonstration has to be drawn from the general idea of history. And this idea should henceforth be simply the idea of a lofty psychology, namely, that the human being should be understood once and for all as an intelligent being in abstraction, but never as the individual and personal being, circumscribed by the present moment, an ephemeral insect, which is born and dies on the same day, and which is linked

190

with the totality of things merely by the law of birth and corruption. Thus, we must show what really makes humanity continue to exist: we must reveal to everyone the mysterious reality, hiding in the depths of intellectual nature and which is still visible only to the eye enlightened by some special illumination. Only let us not be too exclusive, too fanciful, or too symmetrical; but most important, let us speak to our century simply in the language of the century and not in the antiquated language of dogma, which has become unintelligible; then success will undoubtedly be achieved in this today, since reason, science, and even art seem to precipitate passionately towards a new ethical cataclysm, as in the Saviour's great epoch.

I have often spoken to you about the influence which Christian truth exercised upon society. I have not told you everything. Though it is hard to believe this, nonetheless what I am going to say is a completely new matter. Men appreciate the moral influence of Christianity well enough, but they have still scarcely thought about its properly intellectual activity, about the powerful force of its logic. Nothing has been said yet about that role which Christianity played in the development and in the formation of modern thought. Men still do not know that our whole argumentation is Christian; we all still believe that we think in the categories and syllogisms of Aristotle. This is because the long complaints of the philosophers and the schismatics about those centuries,[1] in which there was supposedly only superstition, ignorance, and fanaticism, have forced us to lose sight completely of the beneficial effects of the Christian religion. So, when the fever of skepticism was over, the most righteous and humble minds found themselves alienated upon their own terrain, and only with great effort did they establish anew everything in its place in their idea. Moreover, it is true that these intellectuals[2] are not sufficiently interested in the study of purely human reality. They neglect it too much. Habitually contemplating superhuman activity, they do not see the natural forces working in the world, so they almost completely disregard the material conditions of intellectual activity. But it is time for modern reason to acknowledge that all its power is due to Christianity. It is time for it to learn that it is only through the extraordinary means furnished by revelation and through the living clarity which Christianity was able to spread to all objects of human reflection that the majestic structure of the new science was built. This proud science should, at last, acknowledge by itself that it was elevated so high only thanks to the strict rule, the fixed principle, and, most of all, thanks to this instinct and this passion for truth which science found in the teachings of Christ.

Fortunately we do not live in the times in which partisan obstinacy was taken for conviction and sectarian hatred for fervor.[3] For this reason one can hope that agreement may be reached. But, of course, you will agree that it is not up to the truth to make concessions. And this is not a question of etiquette: for the lawful authority[4] concession would mean renunciation of all power and all influence; it would mean self-destruction. This is not a question of delusion or of any kind of external impression. Every delusion has been dispelled forever, every illusion has been ended forever. We are concerned with a very real thing, more real than it is possible to express in words. It is past existence which warrants future existence; such is the law of life. If you renounce your past you deprive yourself of the future. However, for example, the three hundred years' time which the great Christian error[5] reckons as its own is not simply a memory which can be erased away by wishing for it. For this reason the schismatics can build whatever future they want. From the beginning the old community lived only by hope and by faith in the destinies promised it, whereas the schismatics have lived on to this day without any idea of the future.

But, first of all, there is an essential matter which requires clarification above all. Among the things which promote the preservation of truth on earth, one of the most effective is certainly the sacred book of the New Testament. Men naturally treat the book containing the authentic document for the establishment of the new order on earth with mechanical veneration. The written word does not disappear like the spoken word. The written word coerces the mind. It strictly subordinates the mind to itself by its stability and its long sanction. But at the same time, in codifying reason, the written word deprives it of mobility and confines it by forcing it into the narrow framework of the Scripture, enchaining it in every way. Nothing hinders religious thought in its lofty impulse, in its infinite progress, as much as the book; nothing makes the continual conclusive strengthening of religious thought in the human soul so difficult. Today everything is based upon the letter in the religious sphere, and even the voice of the incarnate reason remains silent. The pulpits of truth resound only with words devoid of will and devoid of authority. The sermon is no longer anything but an incidental affair in the work of salvation. But, finally, you must admit, the discourse transmitted to us in Scripture was, of course, directed simply at those who were there listening. As a result Scripture could not be equally intelligible to men of all times and all places. It has to be marked by a certain local color from the times in which it was written, but this shuts Scripture up in a sphere, from which it can only be released by means of a more or less arbitrary and completely human interpretation. Then how can this old word always address the world with the same power which it had at the time when it was the genuine speech of its own time, the real power of the moment? Does the world not need a new voice in contact with the course of history, a voice whose sounds would not be foreign to any ear and would vibrate equally upon all points on earth, so that the echoes of the present century would seize upon it with the desire to spread it from one end of the world to the other?

The verb, the word addressed to all centuries, is not only just the discourse of the Saviour, it is His whole heavenly image, crowned with His halo, covered with His blood, suspended on the cross, the way God once

placed Him within human memory. When the son of
God said that He would send men the spirit and that
He Himself would be in the midst of them for eternity,
do you really believe that He was thinking about this
book made after His death, in which, for better or
worse, His life and His speeches were related and
some of the speeches by His disciples were collected?
Do you believe that He thought that this book would
perpetuate His teaching on earth? Certainly this was
not His thought. However, he meant that after Him
there would be men, who would become so absorbed
in the contemplation and in the study of His perfec-
tions and would be so filled with His teaching and the
example of His life, that morally they would form *one
whole* with Him and that these men, following each
other through all future ages, would transmit His
whole thought, His whole being from generation to
generation; here is what He wanted to say and here is
what is not understood. It is believed that His whole
heritage is found written in these pages, which have
been deformed so often by so many diverse interpretations and twisted so often by flights of fancy.

As is known, Christianity was consolidated without
the cooperation of any kind of book. In the second century Christianity had already conquered the world.
And from that time onward the human race was subjected irrevocably to it. People imagine that they only
have to disseminate this book throughout the earth in
order to convert the world! A wretched idea on which
the apostates passionately subsist!

It is in men made such as we, made as He was, that

divine reason lives on, not in the volume fabricated by the Church. And that is precisely why the obstinate attachment on the part of traditional people to the astounding dogma of the real presence of the body in the Eucharist and this hyperbolic worship of the body of the Saviour are so admirable. Nothing helps us understand the source of Christian truth better than that: nothing helps us see more clearly the necessity of striving to realize the material presence of the God-man among us in every possible way, by evoking his corporeal image constantly, in order to have this formidable image continually before our eyes as the eternal model and lesson for the new humanity. In my opinion, this fact is worthy of contemplation. This strange dogma of the Eucharist, object of derision and scorn, open to the evil attacks of human argument on so many sides, is still nonetheless preserved indestructibly and purely in the minds of some. Why? Could it not be in order to serve one day as an element of union among the different Christian systems? Could it not be so that one day in the world there would flash some new light, which at present is still hidden with its miraculous destiny? I am certain of it.

Therefore, although the sign traced by human thought should be considered as a necessary element of the moral world, it is nonetheless true that the real basis for the contact of intelligences and for the universal development of rational being is to be found elsewhere: namely, in the living word, in this word which is altered according to the times, lands, and the persons involved but is always remaining what it should be, needing neither commentaries nor exegeses, its authenticity requiring no recourse to any canon, and finally it is to be found in the natural instrument of our thought. So, whereas I would not call it heterodox to assume that all wisdom is contained in the pages of one book, as the schismatics hold, yet it certainly has very little in common with philosophy. And moreover, it is certain that there is a lofty philosophy in these persevering beliefs which compels the people of the law to recognize another purer source of truth, another less earthly authority.

Men must learn to esteem this Christian reason so secure, so exact in these people.[6] It is the instinct for truth, it is the consequence of the moral principle, borne from activity back into the mind; this is the unconscious logic of a perfectly disciplined reasoning. An extraordinary understanding of life, brought into the world by the founder of Christianity, a spirit of abnegation, an aversion to separation, a passionate love for unity: here is what guides the pure Christians in everything. In this way the idea revealed from above is preserved, in this way the grand operation of the fusion of souls and of the world's different moral forces into one soul, into a single force is completed through this idea. This fusion is the whole mission of Christianity. The truth is one: the kingdom of God, heaven on earth, all the promises in the Bible—all this is nothing but the prophecy and the work of the unification of all human thought in a unique thought; and this unique thought is the thought of God Himself, to put it in another way, *the accomplished moral law.*

All the work of the ages in man's intellectual life is meant to produce this definite result which is the end and goal of all things, the last phase of human nature, the dénouement of the universal drama, the grand apocalyptic synthesis.

The *Apologia* of a *Madman*

"Charity," says St. Paul, "suffers everything, believes everything, endures everything."[1] So, let us suffer, believe, and endure everything; let us be charitable. But, first of all, the catastrophe which has just crushed my philosophical existence and thrown the work of an entire life to the winds is simply the necessary result of the cry which arose upon the appearance of my article,[2] of this page which could be considered acrimonious but which certainly merited something besides the outcry which greeted it. After all, the government has only done its duty: it can even be said that the measures which it took in my case were completely liberal, since they did not exceed the expectation of the public. What could the most well-meaning government do other than conform to the general tone?

As for the public outcry, this is something completely different. There are different ways of loving one's country. For example, the Samoyed who loves the native snows which have rendered him near-sighted, the smoky hut in which he remains cowering

199

for half of his life, the rancid grease of his reindeer which surrounds him with a nauseous atmosphere, assuredly does not love his country in the same way as the Englishman, proud of his institutions and of the high civilization in his fortunate island, and it would undoubtedly be quite unfortunate if we were still at the state of cherishing the localities which saw us born in the way that the Samoyeds do.

Love of the fatherland is certainly a very beautiful thing, but there is something better than that; it is the love of truth. Love of fatherland makes heroes, love of truth makes wise men, the benefactors of humanity; it is love of fatherland which divides peoples, which feeds national hatreds, which sometimes covers the earth with mourning; it is love of truth which spreads light, which creates the joys of the spirit, which brings men close to the Divinity. It is not by way of the fatherland, it is by way of the truth that one mounts to heaven. It is true that, as for us Russians, we have few men in love with truth; we lack examples, so one must not expect too much from a nation which has always been so little concerned with what is true and what is not, if it was so affected by a slightly virulent address directed at its infirmities. Moreover, I have no rancor, I assure you, against this dear public which cajoled me for such a long time: it is with composure, without any irritation, that I am trying to explain to myself my strange situation! Must I not try to explain to myself where one upon whom insanity has been imposed stands vis-à-vis his confreres, vis-à-vis his fellow citizens, vis-à-vis his God?

I have never put much stock in the populace; I have never had democratic tastes; I have never courted popular ovations nor esteemed the judgments of the crowd. I have always thought that humanity could advance only by following its elite, by following those who have the mission of leading it; that universal opinion is not absolute reason as a great writer of our times[3] believed, that the instincts of majorities are necessarily more egotistical, more emotional, more narrow than those of the solitary man; that what men call the common sense of the people is not good sense at all; that truth cannot be represented by a number; finally that human intelligence always manifests itself most powerfully only in the solitary mind, center and sun of its sphere. Then how does it happen that one day I found myself faced by an enraged public whose approvals I never earnestly sought, whose favors never pleased me, whose sallies never affected me? How is it that a thought which was not addressed to the world, which, I declared a thousand times, had nothing to do with my contemporaries, which I bequeathed in the depths of my convictions to future generations better informed than we, how is it that with this quality of semipublicity which it had already acquired, this thought had one day broken its fetters, had escaped from its cloister, had precipitated into the street bounding into the midst of the stupefied crowd? Certainly I cannot say why, but here is what I can affirm with a perfect assurance.

For the past three hundred years[4] Russia has been aspiring to identify herself with the West, she has been admitting her inferiority to the West, drawing all her ideas, all her teachings, all her joys from the West. For more than a century Russia has done better than that. The greatest of our kings,[5] our glory, our demigod, he who began a new era for us, he to whom we owe our greatness and all the goods which we possess, renounced old Russia a hundred years ago in front of the entire world. With his powerful breath he swept away all our old institutions: he dug out an abyss between our past and our present, and he threw all our traditions into it; he went to make himself the smallest in the West, and he returned the greatest among us; he prostrated himself before the West, and he rose as our master and our legislator; he introduced Western idioms into our idiom; he molded the letters of our alphabet upon those of the West; he disdained the clothes of our fathers and made us adopt Western dress; he gave his new capital a Western name; he threw away his hereditary title and adopted a Western title; lastly, he renounced his own name and wrote his signature with a Western name. Since that time, our eyes constantly turned towards the West, and we did nothing but inhale the emanations which came to us from there and nourish ourselves on them. As for our princes, who were always in advance of the nation, who always dragged us along the road of perfection in spite of ourselves, who always towed the country behind them, without the country doing anything at all, they themselves imposed Western customs, language, and luxury upon us. We learned how to read from Western books, we learned how to speak from

Westerners; as for our own history, it is the West which taught it to us; we drew everything from the West, we translated the whole West and were finally happy in resembling the West and proud when the West counted us among its own.

This creation of Peter the Great was beautiful, you must agree, this thought of the man of genius who dictated the route which we were henceforth obliged to follow: profound was this word which said to us: Do you see this civilization over there, fruition of so much work, these sciences, these arts, which cost so much sweat for so many generations? All that is yours on condition that you throw off your superstitions, that you repudiate your prejudices, that you will no longer be proud of your barbarous past, that you will ardently desire only to adopt the works of all nations, the riches acquired by the human spirit in all parts of the globe.

And it is not just for his nation alone that the great man worked. Providential men are always sent for the entire universe: a nation demands them first, then they are absorbed into humanity, like these great rivers which first fertilize vast countries, and then go on to flow into the ocean. When forsaking royal majesty and his land, he went to conceal himself in the lowest ranks of civilized people; was it not a unique spectacle, which he offered the universe, of a new effort of man's genius to emerge from narrow sphere of the fatherland, in order to become established in the great sphere of humanity? Such was the lesson which we ought to have gleaned from it! We really did profit from it, and up to this day we have marched along the road which the great emperor mapped out for us. Our immense development is nothing but the fruition of this vast thought. Never has there been a people less infatuated with itself as the Russian people fashioned by Peter the Great. The lofty intelligence of this extraordinary man envisioned completely what ought to be our starting point. He saw that, since we lacked historical data completely, we could not found our future upon this wholly empty basis; he understood that confronted by the old European civilization, all we had to do is choke ourselves in our history, drag ourselves along like the western people across the world of national prejudices, by the narrow lanes of municipal ideas, in order, by means of a spontaneous flight, to deprive ourselves necessarily of the destinies reserved for us. So, he liberated us from all these precedents which encumber historical societies and impede their development; he opened our intelligence to all great and beautiful ideas existing among men; he handed us over totally to the West, such as the centuries have made it, and he gave us all its history for a history, all its future for a future.

Do you believe that if he had found a rich and fertile history, living traditions, enrooted institutions amid his nation, he would not have hesitated to cast the nation into a new world, to divest it of its nationality? On the contrary, would he not have sought the means of regenerating the nation in this nationality itself? And as for the nation, would it have put up with the fact that its past was ravaged, that Europe's was, as it were, imposed upon it?

But such was not the case. In his land Peter the Great found only a blank sheet of paper, and he wrote on it: Europe and West; since then we belonged to Europe and to the West. One must not be mistaken about it: whatever the genius of this man was, his work was possible only within a nation whose precedents were not imperiously governing the development which it had to pursue, whose traditions did not have the faculty of creating a future for it, whose memories could be erased with impunity by an audacious legislator. If we were so docile to the voice of the prince who dragged us into a new life, the reason is that we had nothing in our past existence which could legitimize resistance. The most profound trait of our social physiognomy is spontaneity. Each fact in our history is an isolated fact, an imposed fact; each new idea, a detached idea, an imported idea. Therefore, we naturally lack the link between the event of the day and that of yesterday. But there is nothing in this point of view which could justly offend national sentiment. If it is true, it must be accepted, that is all. Since human logic has been denied us, providential logic watched over us and directed us toward its goals. There are great nations, just as there are great historic personages which cannot be explained by the laws of our reason, but which supreme reason decrees in its mystery: so it is with us. Once again, the national honor has nothing to do with it.

The history of a people is not only a sequence of facts which follow upon one another, but also a series of ideas which are linked together. The fact must be translated by an idea; then you have a history; then the fact is not lost; it has ploughed furrows in the intelligent being, it has remained engraved in men's hearts. This history is not made by the historian, it is the development of things. The historian comes along one day, finds everything completed and relates it: but whether he comes or not, history exists there nonetheless; everyone carried it within the depth of his being. That is precisely the history which we do not have. We must learn to get along without it and not to stone the men who have been the first to become aware of that.

From time to time in their diverse excavations our fanatic Slavicists[6] will, of course, still be able to exhume curios for our museums, for our libraries; but one may doubt if out of the depths of our historical soil they can ever draw something to fill up the emptiness in our souls, something to condense the vacuity in our minds. Look at Europe in the Middle Ages; there is no event which is not there, as it were, because of an absolute necessity. Moreover, how many furrows has this history dug in men's intellects, as it worked over the terrain upon which man's spirit is moving! I know, of course, that all histories do not possess the rigorous and logical development like that of this prodigious epoch, but it is nonetheless true that there is the genuine character of an historical development, whether it be for one people or for a group of people and that the nations deprived of a past formed in this way should seek the basis for their subsequent progress somewhere other than in their memory. It is the same for the life of peoples as for that of individuals; all men have lived, but only the man of genius has a history.

For example, when a people by means of a concourse of circumstances not fashioned by it and by the effect of a geographical position not chosen by it, expands over an immense amount of land without realizing what it is doing and when one day it discovers itself to be a powerful people, this is assuredly a surprising phenomenon and it could be admired in silence, but what can history say about it? The history of this people will begin only from the day on which it will be seized by an idea entrusted to it, one which it is called upon to realize, and the day on which it will begin to pursue the idea with this persevering, though obscure, instinct which leads people to their destinies. That is the moment which I evoke for my country with all the powers of my heart; that is the task which I would like to see us undertake; it is up to you, my dear friends and fellow-citizens, who live in a century of lofty teaching and who have just taught me how inspired you are with the holy love of the fatherland.

Since time immemorial the world has been divided into two spheres, into East and West. That is not simply a geographical division, it is an order of things resulting from the very nature of intelligent being. There are two principles which respond to the two dynamic forces of nature, these are two ideas which embrace the whole economy of mankind. It is through self-concentration, meditation, and withdrawal that the human spirit discovered its powers in the East; it is through expansion to the outside, spreading out in

207

every direction through the fight with all the obstacles, that the human spirit developed in the West. In the East, thought withdrawn within itself, sheltered in its repose, hidden in the desert, left social power as master of all earthly goods; in the West the idea of diffusing itself everywhere, embracing all man's needs, aspiring to all kinds of happiness, based power upon the principle of law. Nonetheless in both of these spheres life was strong and productive; in both, human intelligence did not lack any lofty inspirations, profound thoughts, sublime creations. The East came first and poured waves of light from the depths of its silent meditation; then came the West, with its immense activity, its living word; it became imbued with its works, achieved what the East had begun, and finally enveloped the East in its vast embrace. But in the East, the docile intelligent men, having knelt before the authority of the ages, dissipated themselves in the initial ages of the world by the exercise of their absolute submission and stood one day immobile and dumb without suspecting the new destinies which were being prepared for them; whereas in the West intelligent men marched proud and free, bowing only before the authority of reason and of heaven, halting only before the unknown, with their eyes always fixed upon the boundless future. And there intelligent men still advance, as you know, and you also know that since Peter the Great we believed that we advanced with them.

But here comes a new school[7] into our midst. They do not want anything from the West anymore, they want to demolish the work of Peter the Great; they want to follow the road into the desert once again. Unmindful of what the West has done for us, they insult it; ungrateful towards the great man who regenerated us, towards Europe which taught us, they deny both the great man and Europe and already in its premature ardor this newly-born patriotism proclaims us Eastern. What need have we, they say, to seek enlightenment in the countries of Europe? We ought to have left it up to the passage of time: left to ourselves, we should have undoubtedly surpassed all these people bound to error and to deceit. Then what do we have to envy the West for? The religious wars, the Inquisition, the Pope, the Jesuits? What truly beautiful things! It is not the West, it is the East which is the fatherland of sciences and of vast thoughts. Let us withdraw then into this East which touches us everywhere and from which we lately received our beliefs, our laws, our virtues, all that has rendered us the most powerful people upon the earth. The old East is fading away: well then, we are its natural heirs; it is in our midst that the great and mysterious truths, preserved by the East so long for the good of humanity, are going to be perpetuated.

Now you realize the origins of the hurricane which struck me the other day, and you see that a real reaction is taking place in our land. But this time the impetus does not come from on high. On the contrary, in the upper levels of society never was the memory of our great legislator more venerated than today. Therefore, the initiative belongs wholly to the country.

Where this first act of the emancipated reason of the nation will lead us, God knows! But, if a man earnestly loves his country, he cannot fail to be affected sorrowfully by this apostasy of our most advanced minds in regard to all that was previously our glory, our honor; and it is up to the good citizen to try to evaluate this unusual phenomenon as best he can.

We are situated in eastern Europe, that is positive, but we were never part of the East because of that. The East possesses, as we have just seen, an idea which was inlaid in men's minds since the first days of creation. It is a fertile idea which in its time led to an immense development of intelligent being. The idea established the spiritual principle at the pinnacle of society; it subordinated all powers to a supreme, inviolable law, the law of the times and profoundly understood social hierarchies and, although the idea compressed life into a confined area, it nonetheless removed it from all external influence. All that was completely foreign to us. The spiritual principle never became a factor in our society; the law of the times, tradition, has never reigned in our land; as for social hierarchies, we never had any; and finally life was never independent in our land. We are simply just a northern country, and on the basis of our ideas as much as that of our climates, far removed from the perfumed valley of Kashmir and the sacred shores of the Ganges. True, some of our provinces border on the eastern empires, but our centers are not there, our life is not there and will never be there, unless the earth's axis be displaced or unless a new cataclysm again transform the southern formations into polar ices.

The fact is that we have never yet considered our history from the philosophical point of view; none of the great events of our past life has been depicted well, none of our great epochs has been evaluated in good faith, that is the reason for all our bizarre fantasies. German scholars discovered our annalists fifty years ago;[8] then Karamzin[9] related the facts and feats of our princes in a sonorous style; in our day mediocre writers, who possess neither German science nor the style of the illustrious prose writer, imagine that they can describe times and customs which none of us remember or love: this is the summary of our works in national history.[10] You must agree that from so few things one could never draw something to make a great people sense the destinies awaiting it. But it is precisely that which concerns us today, it is precisely these results which form the whole interest of historical studies in our days. What the earnest thought of the times in which we live requires is a strict meditation, an impartial analysis of the moments in which the people's life is revealed with more or less intensity, for there is the future, there are the elements of its possible development. So, if such epochs are rare in your history, if life in your country was not always powerful and profound, do not shun the truth, do not feed upon lies, do not imagine then that you have lived when you drag yourself from one grave to another, but after that, if throughout this nothingness you come to a moment in which the nation began to feel itself living earnestly, in which its heart began to beat and if you hear the sound of the popular wave catching hold and mounting around you, then stop, meditate, study; your efforts will not be in vain. You will learn what your country can do in days of greatness, what it can hope for in the future. In our land, for example, such was the moment which ended the terrible drama of the interregnum,[11] when the nation, after having vanquished its enemy by itself, raised upon its shield the noble house which reigns over us, a unique moment and one which cannot be admired enough if you consider the emptiness of the preceding centuries and the very special situation of our fatherland. It is evident that I am far from demanding, as people have assumed, that violent hands should be laid upon all our memories: I only say that it is time to glance lucidly upon our past, and to do it, not in order to extract old relics fallen into decay, old ideas which time has devoured, old antipathies which the good sense of our princes long since refuted, but in order to learn what we should know about our past. This is what I tried to do in a work which has remained incomplete,[12] and in the piece which recently aroused national pride in such a strange way was supposed to serve as an introduction to it.[13] This initial spirit of a vividly felt idea was undoubtedly too passionate, there was undoubtedly a lack of patience in the expression, some excess at the basis of the thought, but the emotion which dominates the whole piece is not at all hostile to the fatherland; it is a somber sadness expressed in vehement words, nothing more.

More than anyone at all, believe me, I love my

country dearly, I am ambitious for its glory, I know how to esteem the eminent qualities of my nation, but it is true that the patriotic sentiment which animates me is not formed exactly like that of the men whose cries upset my obscure existence and launched my barge, beached at the foot of the cross, onto their ocean of miseries. It is true that I have not learned to love my fatherland with my eyes closed, forehead bowed, mouth closed. I find that one can be useful to one's country only on the condition that one sees things clearly; I believe that the times of blind loves are over, that fanaticisms of any kind are no longer in season: I love my country in the way that Peter the Great taught me to love it. I do not possess, I admit, this sanctimonious patriotism, this lazy patriotism which manages to see everything as beautiful, which slumbers upon its illusions, and which has unfortunately afflicted many of our good minds today. I think that if we have come after the others, it is in order to do better than the others, in order not to fall into their superstitions, into their blindnesses, into their infatuations. To reduce us to repeating the long series of follies and calamities which nations less favored than ours had to undergo would be, in my opinion, a strange misunderstanding of the role which has been allotted to us. I find that our situation is a fortunate one, provided that we know how to evaluate it, and that the ability to contemplate and to judge the world from the heights of a thought freed from unbridled passions, from miserable interests which encroach upon it, is a lovely privilege. There is more: I have the inner conviction that we are called upon to resolve most of the problems in the social order, to accomplish most of the ideas which arose in the old societies, to make a pronouncement about those very grave questions which preoccupy humanity. I have often said, and I love to repeat it, that by the very force of circumstances we have been constituted as a genuine jury for countless trials being handled before the great tribunals of the world.

See what is really taking place today in these countries which I have perhaps praised too much, but which are nonetheless the most complete models of all kinds of civilization. There when a new idea occurs, all the egoisms, vanities, and partialities on the surface of society throw themselves upon it, seize hold of it, disfigure it, make a travesty of it, and a moment later, pulverized by these diverse agents, there it lies, transported into the abstract regions in which all the sterile dusts of the human mind are accumulated. In our land, there are none of these passionate interests, these already-formed opinions, these inveterate prejudices: we approach each new truth with virgin minds. In our institutions, spontaneous works of our princes, in our customs which possess just a century of existence, in our opinions which still seek to become fixed upon the most insignificant things, nothing opposes the good things which Providence destines for humanity. It is enough for a sovereign will to be pronounced among us, in order to have all our opinions disappear, to have all our beliefs waver, to have all our minds open up to the new thought offered to them. Perhaps it would have been better to pass through all the trials experienced by the other Christian people, to draw from them as they did, powers, energies, new methods and perhaps our isolated position would have preserved us from the calamities which accompanied the long education of these peoples, but that is not the issue now; what we have to do is simply to understand properly the present character of our country as it is given to us, as it is irrevocably fixed by the nature of things, and to draw all possible profit from it. History is no longer ours, it is true, but science is ours; we could not begin the whole work of humanity again, but we can participate in its latest works. This past is no longer within our powers, but the future belongs to us.

There is no possible doubt about it, the world is oppressed by its tradition; let us not envy the world for the limited circle in which it flounders; it is certain that in the heart of all the nations there is a deep feeling of their life of past accomplishments which dominates their present life, an obstinate memory of days gone by which fills their todays. Let them struggle with their inexorable past. We have never lived under the rule of historical necessities; never did an omnipotent law precipitate us into the abysses which the times dig in front of nations. Today let us not go and deliver ourselves over to these somber fatalities which we never experienced: let us rejoice in the immense advantage of being able to march forward with the awareness of the route which we have to travel, by obeying only the voice of enlightened reason with a deliberate will. Let us realize that for us there exists no absolute necessity, that we are not, thank God, situated on the rapid slope which sweeps the other people towards the destinies of which they are unaware; that it is given to us to measure each step which we make, to reason our each idea which happens to graze our intellect, that we are permitted to aspire to types of prosperity which are vaster than the prosperity of which the most ardent ministers of the religion of progress dream, and that, in order to achieve definite results, we need only a powerful will, like the one which regenerated us recently.

Well then, is that a shabby future which I offer to my fatherland? Are those gloryless destinies which I evoke for it? However, this great future which will be realized, these beautiful destinies which will be accomplished, will undoubtedly simply be the result of this special nature of the Russian people which was pointed out in the fatal article.[14] But what was this article really? It was an intimate letter written to a woman many years ago under the impact of a painful sentiment, of an immense disappointment which the indiscreet vanity of a journalist turned over to the public, a letter which, read and reread a thousand times before publication and much harsher in the original than in the weak translation in which it appeared, never provoked ill feeling from anyone at all, not even from the most patriotic idolators; finally in the letter, amid some pages of a profound devotion an historical study was inserted in which the old thesis of the superiority of western countries was reproduced with a certain warmth, perhaps with some exaggeration. Such was this detestable writing, this incendiary pamphlet which attracted public anger, the strangest of persecutions upon the author.

Yet, I am anxious to state and am happy to have been led to make this admission: yes, there was some exaggeration in this type of indictment against a great people, whose only crime, in the last analysis, consisted in having been relegated to the extremities of the civilized world, far from the centers in which all the lights naturally had to accumulate, far from the sources from which they shined forth for centuries; there was some exaggeration in not acknowledging that we came into the world upon a sterile soil upon which empires did not flourish, which generations did not venerate, where nothing spoke to us about ages gone by, upon which there was no vestige of previous civilizations, no reminder, no monument of the world which has disappeared; there was some exaggeration in not giving credit to this Church which was so humble, so heroic sometimes, which alone consoles us for the emptiness of our annals, and which deserves the honor for every act of courage, for every beautiful devotion of our fathers; finally, there was undoubtedly some exaggeration in momentarily despairing of a nation which carries in its loins the great soul of Peter the Great. But, after all, you must also agree that the caprices and fancies of our public are unintelligible.

Remember that a few days before the publication which concerns us, a new play was performed in our theater, in which, an unheard-of thing happened: the cutting satire of our customs evidently produced

almost tragic emotion.[15] Well, never was a nation casti-
gated in such a way, never was a country dragged
through the mud, never has so much excrement been
thrown in the face of the public and never, however,
was a success more complete.

Notes

NOTES TO THE BIOGRAPHICAL SKETCH

1. The best book containing biographical materials on Chaadaev is Charles Quénet's *Tchaadaev et les lettres philosophiques* (Paris, 1931). See also Mikhail O. Gershenzon, *P. Ya. Chaadaev: Zhizn i myshlenie* (St. Petersburg, 1908); Alexander von Shelting, *Russland und Europa im russischen Geschichtsdenken* (Bern, 1948); Martin Winkler, *Peter Jakŏlevič Čaadaev, Ein Beitrag zur russischen Geistesgeschichte des 19. Jahrhunderts* (Berlin-Koenigsberg, 1927); Heinrich Falk, *Das Weltbild Peter J. Tschaadajews nach seinen acht "Philosophischen Briefen"* (Munich, 1954); Eugene Moskoff, *The Russian Philosopher Chaadayev, His Ideas and His Epoch*, Columbia University dissertation (New York, 1937); P. S. Shkurinov, *P. Ya. Chaadaev. Zhizn, Deyatelnost, Mirovozzrenie* (Moscow, 1960).

2. Mikhail N. Longinov (1823–1875), a contemporary of Chaadaev's favored the year 1793 as Chaadaev's birthdate. See his articles: "Nekrolog Petra Yakovlevicha Chaadaeva 1793–1856," *Sovremennik*, Vol. LVIII, Section 5, 1856; "Sovremennaya Letopis," *Russkii Vestnik*, Vol. II, 1860, p. 153; "Vospominaniya o P. Ya. Chaadaeve," *Russkii Vestnik*, Vol. XI, 1862. Dmitri N. Sverbeev (1799–1874), who knew Chaadaev personally, wrote a long article about him in *Russkii Arkhiv*, Vol. VI, 1868, pp. 976–1001; in this article he stated that Chaadaev was born in the first years of the "final decade of the eighteenth century"; this same article was republished at the end of the second volume of Sverbeev's memoirs entitled *Zapiski D. N. Sverbeeva*, Vol. II (St. Petersburg, 1899), pp. 235 ff. However, Sverbeev's book is filled with factual errors, so that all his statements have to be checked against other source

materials. Mikhail I. Zhikharev, Chaadaev's nephew, gives 1796 as the year is which Chaadaev was born; see his "P. Ya. Chaadaev, Iz Vospominani Sovremennika," *Vestnik Evropy*, Vols. VII and IX, 1871. Mikhail Lemke set Chaadaev's birthdate as May 27, 1793, in his article on Chaadaev which appeared in *Mir Bozhii*, Vol. IX, 1905, p. 2. See also M. Lemke, *Nikolaevskie Zhandarmy i literatura, 1825–1855* (St. Petersburg, 1908), p. 362. Gershenzon fixed the date as May 27, 1794, in his biography *P. Ya. Chaadaev: Zhizn i myshlenie*, p. 4. Vasili Chistyakov's article "K biografi Petra Yakovlevicha Chaadaeva," *Russkaya Starina*, Vol. 8, 1907, pp. 333–334, added new evidence but did not clear up the controversy. See also A. V. Zvenigorodskoi "Reestr roda Chaadaevykh," *Sbornik Nizhegorodskoi Universiteta. Arkhivnyi Komissii*, Vol. VIII, Part 3, pp. 400–403. Details on this question are to be found in Quénet, pp. lxv–lxviii.

3. Quénet, pp. lviii–lxiii.

4. *Ibid.*, p. 3.

5. Zhikharev, Vol. VII, p. 181.

6. In *Russkaya Starina*, Chistyakov claimed that in *Moskovskie Vedomosti*, No. 54, 1808, he found the names of Mikhail and Peter Chaadaev inscribed on the books of the University in September, 1808. See Chistyakov, p. 334.

7. Dmitri Shakhovskoi, "P. Ya. Chaadaev na puti v Rossiiu v 1826 g." *Literaturnoe nasledstvo*, Vols. 19–21 (Moscow, 1935), p. 31. Hereafter referred to as *Lit. nasled.*

8. *Ibid.*

9. There have been conflicting accounts of the Troppau incident. Sverbeev's biographical article (cited above) is full of error. He claimed that Chaadaev procrastinated during the trip from St. Petersburg to Troppau and that

Chaadaev was dismissed from the army because of this. Longinov (cited above) proved this false and showed that Chaadaev was actually in line for a promotion to aide-de-camp of Emperor Alexander himself. On January 2, 1821, Chaadaev wrote to his aunt: "The fact is that I was supposed to be appointed aide-de-camp to the emperor upon his return, at least that is what Vasilchikov said; I considered it more amusing to scorn this favor, rather than to receive it. It was amusing to show my scorn to people who scorn everybody. So there you are, all that is extraordinarily simple." P. Ya. Chaadaev, "Letter to Princess Anna Mikhailovna Scherbatova, January 2, 1821," *Sochineniya i Pisma P. Ya. Chaadaeva,* Gershenzon edition, Vol. I (Moscow, 1913), p. 4. Hereafter referred to as Chaadaev, *Soch.* (Gersh. ed.). This statement explains the request for discharge well enough, but it does not clarify why Chaadaev was not advanced in grade upon discharge as was usual in cases of this type.

10. Shakhovskoi, "Neizdannye 'Filosoficheskie Pisma' P. Ya. Chaadaeva," *Lit. nasled.,* Vols. 22–24, (Moscow, 1935), p. 13.

11. Shakhovskoi, *Lit. nasled.,* Vols. 19–21, pp. 16–33; also B. M. Fikh "P. Ya. Chaadaev v Breste," *Istoriya SSSR,* Vol. I (Moscow, 1958), p. 177.

12. N. Golitsyn, "Chaadaev i E. A. Sverbeeva," *Vestnik Evropy,* No. 1/4 (Petrograd, 1918), pp. 233–250.

13. *Ibid.*

14. See Chaadaev, *Soch.* (Gersh. ed.), Vol. I, pp. 61–239.

15. Alexander S. Pushkin, "Letter of July 6, 1831 to Chaadaev," *Sochineniya Pushkina,* V. I. Saitova edition (St. Petersburg, 1906–1911), Vol. II, p. 268. See also A. S. Pushkin, *Polnoe Sobranie Sochineni,* Vol. X (Moscow–Leningrad, 1951), p. 174, note 424.

16. The newly found documentation in the manuscript section of the Institute of Russian Literature (Pushkinski Dom) in Leningrad substantiates this fact. Professor Kirpichnikov found an official document relating to this in the Ryumyantsev Museum in Moscow. The document was dated January 31, 1833. The committee on censorship from the Troitski Academy read Letters VI and VII and found that the former letter showed an adverse interpretation of the Russian orthodox religion and the latter letter presented Moses not as a man sent from God, but simply as a great lawgiver. For these and other reasons the committee refused to allow these letters to be published. See A. Kirpichnikov "P. Ya. Chaadaev (po novym dokumentam)," *Russkaya Mysl*, No. 4, 1896, pp. 142–155. Among the Chaadaev papers at the Institute of Russian Literature, after the manuscript of Letter VIII there is a summary of it entitled "Courte analyse et Extraits des Lettres Philosophiques." The "objectionable" sections in all the "Philosophical Letters" are cited there by some unknown censor. In that document among other points, Chaadaev's works are found to contain arguments of liberalism, "St. Simonianism converted to Christianity," and heterodox Christian views; other statements are branded anti-Orthodox and pro-Catholic. Sobranie Dashkova, 93/3/1355, Manuscript Division, Institute of Russian Literature, Academy of the U.S.S.R., Leningrad.

17. Lemke, p. 428.

18. *Ibid.*, pp. 426–428, 443.

19. After the publication of "The First Philosophical Letter," Count Benckendorf prepared the following note for the governor-general of Moscow, Prince Golitsyn (Tsar Nicholas I added "very good" in his own handwriting to the text):

The periodical *Telescope* had published in its last issue (No. 15) an article entitled "The Philosophical Letter," its author is M. Cheodaev [sic] who resides in Moscow. This article, undoubtedly already known to your Excellency, has aroused universal amazement among the inhabitants of Moscow. The author speaks of Russia, of the Russian people, their ideas, religion, and history with such contempt that it is inconceivable how a Russian could degrade himself to such an extent as to write things of that sort. But the residents of our ancient capital, always known for their clear, common sense and filled with the feeling of the dignity of the Russian nation, have at once realized that such an article could not have been written by a compatriot of theirs fully in possession of a sound mind and therefore —as we are informed—they not only did not turn their indignation against M. Cheodaev, but, on the contrary, they expressed their sincere regret on account of the mental derangement with which he was affected and which was the only reason for writing such nonsense. News has been received here that the sympathy on account of M. Cheodaev's unfortunate condition is shared by the entire Moscow public. It is therefore His Imperial Majesty's wish that your Excellency undertake the necessary means to supply M. Cheodaev with medical care and attention. His Imperial Majesty orders you to entrust an able physician with M. Cheodaev's treatment and instruct the physician to visit M. Cheodaev absolutely every morning. An order should also be issued to the effect that M. Cheodaev should not expose himself to the harmful influence of the present damp and cold weather, in short that all necessary steps be taken to have his health improved. His Imperial Majesty wants you to send him a monthly report on M. Cheodaev's condition.

Cited in Lemke, pp. 412–413.

20. Zhikharev, Vol. IX, p. 31.

21. *Ibid.*

22. A. Tseitlin, *Russkaya literatura pervoi poloviny, XIX-ogo veka* (Moscow, 1940), p. 245.

23. Herzen wrote:

That letter was in a sense the last word, the dividing point. It was a shot that rang out in the dark night; whether it was something perishing that proclaimed its end, whether it was a signal or a cry for help, whether it heralded the dawn or foretold that it would never be—anyway, it forced all to awaken.

What, one may wonder, is the significance of two or three pages published in a monthly review? And yet such is the strength of utterance, such is the power of the spoken word in a land of silence, unaccustomed to free speech, that Chaadaev's letter shook all thinking Russia. And well it might. There had been nothing written since *Woe from Wit* which made so powerful an impression. Between that play and the letter there had been ten years of silence, the Fourteenth of December, the gallows, penal servitude, Nicholas.

Memoirs (trans. Constance Garnett) Vol. II, Part IV (London, 1927), pp. 261–262. *Woe from Wit* is the title of a famous play by Alexander Griboedov. The Fourteenth of December refers to the Decembrist uprising of 1825.

24. Similar relaxations took place in the case of the actions taken against the other men involved in the *Telescope* scandal. The censor Boldyrev who had passed on the "First Philosophical Letter" supposedly while playing cards, though dismissed, was allowed to pay a fine of 1,000 rubles, in order to restore himself to full rights for a complete pension. Nikolai Nadezhdin (1802–1856), though exiled to Vologda, was pardoned within a year and received back into government service. He even served as Director of the *Journal of the Ministry of Public Education* later in life. See Quénet, p. 257.

25. Chaadaev, *Soch.* (Gersh. ed.), Vol. I, pp. 288–304.

See also Shakhovskoi, "Proekt Proklamatsi Chaadaeva,"
Lit. nasled., Vol. 22–24, pp. 679–682.

26. Quénet, p. 388.

27. According to Professor Chistyakov, in the baptismal
and birth records of the Moscow Ecclesiastical Consistory,
in No. 131914 one finds the following:

> In the baptismal and birth book of the Moscow Peter-
> Paul Church on Novaya Basmannaya Street, 1856, No.
> 6, is written: April 14 the retired Captain Peter Yakov-
> levich Chaadaev died, in the house of the foreigner
> Shultz, 62 years of age, from an inflammation. The
> parish priest Nicholas Sergicvski heard his confession
> and gave him communion, he also performed the burial
> service. . . . Chistyakov, pp. 333–335.

28. Aleksei S. Khomyakov, *Sochineniya A. S. Khomya-
kova,* Lebedev edition (Moscow, 1878) p. 768.

NOTES TO THE ANALYSIS OF IDEAS

1. The tendency to characterize Chaadaev's thought through the use of old socio-political terminology has led to two "legends." One group of writers has held that Chaadaev was a revolutionary thinker and the other that he was a reactionary thinker. It was Chaadaev's contemporary Alexander Herzen who placed Chaadaev in the revolutionary camp. See Alexander Ivanovich Herzen, "Du développement des idées révolutionnaires en Russie," *Polnoe sobranie sochinenii i pisem*. Lemke edition (Petrograd, 1919 ff.), Vol. VI, p. 317. This same line of thought was taken up by Georgii Plekhanov in "Pessimizn kak otrazhenie ekonomicheskoi deistvitelnosti," *Sochineniya*, Vol. X, 2nd edition (Moscow-Leningrad, 1925), pp. 133–162. The Herzen appraisal has been carried to extremes by Soviet writers. Nikolai Alekseev proclaimed that the First Philosophical Letter contained "in embryo the entire Russian Revolution, the whole of communism, and the International"; see *Russkoe zapadnichestvo* (Moscow, 1929). The standard Soviet line is to treat Chaadaev as an advocate of bourgeois freedom. By "advocate of bourgeois freedom" the Soviets mean that Chaadaev was against serfdom and tsarist absolutism. In his article "Chaadaev i ego filosoficheskie pisma," *Pod znamenem marksizma*, Vol. I (January, 1938) p. 38, V. Soloviev took this line and also emphasized the "social" aspects of Chaadaev's religious thought. See also M. K. Afanasev, "Obshchestvennopoliticheskie vzglyady P. Ya. Chaadaeva," *Trudy voronezhskogo gosudarstvennogo universiteta*, Vol. XIV (1947), pp. 141–156; F. P. Berelevich, "P. Ya. Chaadaev i Dekabristy," *Uchenye zapiski tyumenskogo pedagogicheskogo instituta*, Vol. V (Tyumen, 1958), pp. 157–178; and M. M. Grigorian, "Chaadaev i ego filosoficheskaya sis-

tema," *Sbornik. Iz istorii filosofii* (Moscow, 1958), pp.
126–183. The most recent Soviet effort is a monograph:
P. S. Shkurinov, *P. Ya. Chaadaev. Zhizn, deyatelnost i
mirovozzrenie* (Moscow, 1960). This monograph is mainly
a polemic against Western historians' work on Chaadaev;
the major virtue of the work consists in specific references
to unpublished source materials on Chaadaev. Chaadaev
is depicted as a "progressive, aristocratic revolutionary."
    The opposite "legend" of Chaadaev as a reactionary was
fostered by Alexander N. Pypin who wrote: "In a word,
alongside the contemporary movements of European
thought, Chaadaev's theory appears close to the Catholic
doctrine which was more a reactionary than a progressive one"; *Kharakteristiki literaturnykh mnenii ot dvadt-
satykh do pyatidesyatykh godov*, 4th edition (St. Petersburg, 1909), p. 189. Paul Milyukov supported this thesis
by tracing the influence of the ultramontanist de Maistre
and especially de Bonald in Chaadaev's works; *Glavnyya
techeniya russkoi istoricheskoi mysli*, 3rd edition, (St.
Petersburg, 1913), pp. 323–342. But it was Mikhail O.
Gershenzon who tried to lay to rest the "legend" of
Chaadaev as a revolutionary once and for all. Unfortunately in so doing Gershenzon constructed another "legend" about Chaadaev; Gershenzon thought that he saw
in Chaadaev a Roman Catholic manqué and social mystic.
P. Ya. Chaadaeva: Zhizn i myshlenie (St. Petersburg,
1908).
    Most Western historians have been hampered by lack
of contact with all the manuscript materials in Russian
archives: the most scholarly and exhaustive treatment is
the Herculean biographical study by Charles Quénet,
Tchaadaev et les lettres philosophiques (Paris, 1931).
Quénet gathered much material from the archives, but
unfortunately copies of the five newly discovered "Philo-

sophical Letters" reached him at a very late stage in his research, so that he devoted only two pages to a summary of their contents. Quénet's appraisal of Chaadaev is vague and ambiguous, but all scholars are indebted to him for his meticulous spadework on biographical materials. All other works by historians have depended upon Russian translations of the documents presented by Shakhovskoi; see Alexander von Schelting, *Russland und Europa im russischen Geschichtsdenken* (Bern, 1948); V. Zenkovski, *A History of Russian Philosophy*, trans. George Kline (New York, 1953); Alexandre Koyré, *Etudes sur l'histoire de las pensée philosophique en Russie* (Paris, 1950). Heinrich Falk *(Das Weltbild Peter J. Tschaadajews nach seinen acht "Philosophischen Briefen"* [Munich, 1954]) also labored under the handicap of inaccessibility of the original French texts of the "Philosophical Letters." Falk basically supported the Gershenzon interpretation of Chaadaev.

Two recent works on Russian intellectual history have cast doubts upon the "Christian" nature of Chaadaev's insights. Georgi Florovski has stated that "Chaadaev's image has remained unclear up to this time. And the most unclear fact in him is his religiosity"; *Puti russkogo bogosloviya* (Paris, 1937) p. 247. To Florovski, Chaadaev is "an ideologue not a member of the church. That is the cause of a certain strange obscurity in his historical schema" (p. 248). Peter Scheibert has branded Chaadaev's philosophy of history as "Historiosophia" and "definitely a post-Christian ideology"; *Von Bakunin zu Lenin. Geschichte der russischen revolutionären Ideologien, 1840–1895*, Vol. I (Leiden, 1956).

The terms *revolutionary, reactionary, mystic, progressive,* and *post-Christian ideologue* are not useful in clarifying Chaadaev's thought. This is why I have applied new terms which seem more in keeping with Chaadaev's own aims and ideals. By "utopian" in this context I mean one who believes in the possibility of social regeneration and the perfectibility of society. By "religious" I refer to one who believes religion to be the basis for this social regeneration, and by "social and cultural" I mean one who emphasizes the necessity for establishing proper material conditions in society in order for men to progress intellectually and spiritually.

2. Gershenzon termed Chaadaev a "social mystic," but he based his major argument on the "Memoire zur Geistkunde," which he attributed to Chaadaev. In reality, as Shakhovskoi has shown conclusively, the mystic journal was not written by Chaadaev but by the Moscow doctor, D. A. Obleukhov (See *Literaturnoe nasledstvo,* Vol. 22–24 [Moscow, 1935], p. 12).

Gershenzon concluded that "by the kingdom of God is meant not the general welfare and not the triumph of the moral law but solely and undoubtedly the inner fusion of mankind with God"; *P. Ya. Chaadaev: Zhizn i myshlenie,* p. 76. But Chaadaev's own words contradict this opinion; in writing to Alexander Ivanovich Turgenev, Chaadaev emphasized the real effects of religion upon concrete material conditions: *Le principe du catholicisme est un principe d'action, un principe social avant tout";* in a letter to Circourt Chaadaev wrote: *"Il ne s'agit ici que de notre développement social."* Chaadaev's kingdom of God was not to be a mystical fusion of man with God but a concrete materialization in society. As Koyré put it: "It is God's reign on earth, not the heavenly kingdom, which is at the center of Chaadaev's thought"; *La pensée philosophique en Russie,* p. 37.

3. Pypin, p. 192.

4. On Official Nationality see Nicholas Riasanovsky,

Nicholas I and Official Nationality in Russia, 1825–1855 (Berkeley and Los Angeles, 1959).

5. Nikolai Karamzin wrote:

Situated in the depths of the north, rearing her head between Asiatic and European kingdoms, Russian society contained elements derived from both these parts of the world. It was a compound of ancient customs of the East, carried to Europe by the Slavs and reactivated, so to say, by our long connection with the Mongols; of Byzantine custom which we had adopted together with Christianity; and of certain German customs, imparted to us by the Normans. *Memoir on Ancient and Modern Russia,* translated by Richard Pipes (Cambridge, Mass., 1959), p. 110.

6. Chaadaev's view could be contrasted with the contemporary views of Official Nationalists such as Shevyrev or Pogodin, or else those of the pre-Slavophile, Vladimir Odoevski, the leading light of the *Lyubomudrye.* The theory of "young Russia" as the possible savior of "old Europe" can be found in the idealist circles of the 1820's. See P. Sakulin, *Iz russkogo idealizma* (Moscow, 1913), pp. 613–614. Florovski suggests that Odoevski might have influenced Chaadaev in this line of thinking (p. 248).

7. See Alexandre Koyré, "Russia's Place in the World: Peter Chaadayev and the Slavophils," *The Slavonic Review,* March, 1927, pp. 594–608.

8. See Chaadaev's long attack on the anti-Petrine school in his *Apologia of a Madman.* Professor Riasanovsky in characterizing the Slavophile movement wrote: "The Slavophile denunciation of Peter the Great came to be regarded as the watchword of the movement, as its most characteristic trait and as its main contrast with the Westernizers"; *Russia and the West in the Teachings of the Slavophiles* (Cambridge, Mass., 1952), p. 80.

EXPLANATORY NOTES TO THE
PHILOSOPHICAL LETTERS

LETTER I

1. A letter written by Ekatrina D. Panova to Peter Chaadaev in which she expressed her religious anxieties and also her fears that Chaadaev had suspicions about her real motives in talking with him about religious topics. Since Panova's letter is a help in understanding the text of "The First Philosophical Letter," the following is a translation of it from the original French text; the Gershenzon edition left out the postscript. Unfortunately the letter is not dated. The original is in the manuscript division of the Lenin library in the collection Zhikharev i Chaadaev. M.S.1032/41, "Pisma Panovoi, Ekateriny Dmitrievny k Chaadaevu, Petru Yakovlevichu."

For quite a long time, sir, I longed to write to you, the fear of being troublesome, the idea that you no longer have any interest in what concerns me, made me hesitate, but at last I have nonetheless resolved to send you this letter which will probably be the last which you will receive from me.

Unfortunately I see that I have lost the good will which you showed to me before; you believe, I know, that there was some fakery on my part in the desire which I manifested to you to instruct myself in religious subject matter: I find this thought intolerable. Undoubtedly I have many faults, but never, I assure you, has the idea of pretending ever had a place in my heart for a moment. I saw you so entirely absorbed in religious ideas that it is my admiration, my profound esteem for your character, which inspired in me the need to devote myself to the same thoughts as you. It was with all the warmth, all the enthusiasm of my character that I gave myself over to sentiments which were so new to me. In hearing you speak, I believed; it seemed to me in these

233

moments that nothing was missing for my complete belief, but then when I found myself alone, I got my doubts back; I experienced remorses for inclining towards the Catholic faith; I told myself that I had no conviction other than that of repeating to myself that you could not be wrong—this was really what made the greatest impression upon my belief and this motive was purely human. Believe me, Sir, when I assure you that all these different emotions which I do not have the strength to abate have *considerably* altered my health; I was in a continual state of agitation and always dissatisfied with myself, I must have appeared extravagant and exaggerated to you very often . . . . you naturally have a lot of severity in your character . . . . I noted that lately you have removed yourself even more from our society, but I did not guess your motive. A *word* which *you spoke to my husband* enlightened me on this matter. I could not tell you how much I suffered in thinking of the opinion which you gave of me; it was the cruel but just punishment for the disdain which I have always had for the opinion of the world . . . . But it is time to finish this letter; may it be able to attain its goal, that of convincing you that I have not pretended anything, that I did not think to play a role in order to merit your friendship, that if I have lost your esteem, nothing in the world could compensate me for this loss, not even the sentiment that I have done nothing which could have brought this misfortune upon me. Farewell, Sir; if you would write me a few words in response, I would be very happy, but I really do not dare to expect any.

P.S. My husband is sorry that he cannot return the money to you right away, he is doing all that he can to obtain it, but I doubt whether he will succeed before a month or six weeks pass.

2. John 27:20–21.

3. Chaadaev probably refers to his ideas of the early history of the Eastern Slavs.

4. The early Kievan period.

5. The period of the Tatar yoke.

6. The Muscovite period of Russian history. In this last assumption, Chaadaev apparently held that the Muscovite autocratic form of government grew out of the Tatar rule in Russia.

7. Peter the Great (1682–1725) introduced a series of reforms aimed at "Westernization" of the Russian gentry and the Russian form of government.

8. Alexander I (1801–1825); the reference is to Russia's participation in the wars against Napoleon and to the march of Russian troops into Paris on April 1, 1814.

9. The Decembrist uprising in 1825. A group of Russian nobles, inspired by western European rationalist ideas, led a revolt against tsardom which failed.

10. The migration of the barbarians in the early Middle Ages and the spread of Christianity. To Chaadaev "modern civilization" means "Christian civilization," i.e., European history since the birth of Christ.

11. In the late tenth century, the Russian ruler Vladimir officially adopted Byzantine Christianity.

12. For information on Photius and the temporary, supposed "split" of Eastern and Western Church, see Francis Dvornik, *The Photian Schism* (Cambridge, England, 1948).

13. During the period of the Tatar yoke, Russia lay under Mongol domination from 1240 to 1480.

14. The gradually increasing imposition of serfdom upon the Russian peasant after the end of the Mongol Yoke with the rise of the Muscovite state in the sixteenth century.

15. The flowering of mediaeval culture in western Europe during the late Middle Ages.

16. The Renaissance.

17. The Pope in Rome.

18. In Chaadaev's *Weltanschauung*, Russia had had no Middle Ages like those of Western Europe; furthermore, Russia had had no Renaissance, because she had been completely out of contact with western European culture at the time.

19. Torquato Tasso (1554–1595) wrote the famous epic poem *La Gerusalemme Liberata* which dealt with the Crusades.

20. Chaadaev refers to the initial history of the spread of Christianity as the first epoch of "modern," that is, Christian, civilization, the period up to about the fifth century.

21. Roughly the period from the sixth to the tenth century.

22. Roughly the tenth and eleventh centuries.

23. Roughly the twelfth, thirteenth, and fourteenth centuries.

24. The period before and after the Protestant Reformation; the fifteenth and sixteenth centuries.

25. The eighteenth century Rationalists held this interpretation. Chaadaev is probably thinking of Voltaire's opinion of the Middle Ages. See especially Voltaire's *Essai sur les moeurs* which was found in Chaadaev's personal library.

26. Another reference to eighteenth-century Rationalism and its view of mediaeval history.

27. The English revolution in the latter half of the seventeenth century. In the first volume of his *Histoire de Charles Ier*, the French historian Guizot, whom Chaadaev admired, undoubtedly gave Chaadaev the inspiration for this interpretation. In the Chaadaev manuscript at the top of the page on which these phrases are found, there is a

citation in Russian which reads "in Russian in the translation 'Cromwell and Charles I.' "

28. The Catholic Emancipation Act of 1829 which extended political liberty, including the right to vote, to Roman Catholics in England.

29. The city of the dead, i.e., Moscow.

1. These images are to be found in Plato's Dialogues, in particular, the *Phaedrus* and the *Symposium.* In the *Phaedrus* Socrates exclaims:

By here, a fair resting-place, full of summer sounds and scents. Here is this lofty and spreading plane-tree, and the agnus castus high and clustering, in the fullest blossom and the greatest fragrance; and the stream which flows beneath the plane-tree is deliciously cold to the feet. Judging from the ornaments and images, this must be a spot sacred to Achelous and the Nymphs. How delightful is the breeze: so very sweet; and there is a sound in the air shrill and summerlike which makes answer to the chorus of the cicadae. But the greatest charm of all is the grass, like a pillow gently sloping to the head. My dear Phaedrus, you have been an admirable guide.

The Works of Plato, selected and edited by Irwin Edman (New York: Modern Library, Random House, 1928), p. 267.

In the *Symposium* one finds: "Socrates took his place on the couch, and supped with the rest; and then libations were offered, and after a hymn had been sung to the god, and there had been the usual ceremonies, they were about to commence drinking . . . ." *(The Works of Plato,* p. 338). Chaadaev's private library, partially preserved in the Lenin Library, Moscow, contains a German translation of Plato's works with commentary by Schleiermacher. See also Shakhovskoi, *Literaturnoe nasledstvo,* Vol. 22–24 (Moscow, 1935).

2. "Sleep."

3. Chaadaev definitively attacks serfdom in Russia.

4. See the first paragraphs of "The First Philosophical Letter."

5. Aristotle's *Politics,* Book I, Chapters 4–6.

6. Boris Godunov was regent from 1587 to 1598, during the latter reign of Fedor Ivanovich. When the male line of the Riurik dynasty died out with the death of Tsar Fedor Ivanovich in 1598, Boris Godunov ruled as tsar from 1598 to 1605. Vasili Ivanovich Shuisky seized the throne in 1606 and ruled until 1610. Ivan IV had set a legal prohibition on the movement of peasants during economically critical years. Boris Godunov and Vasili Shuisky added further restrictions which contributed to the development of serfdom.

7. The Russians blockaded the Bosphorus in May, 1829; the reference to the Euphrates is directed at the seizure of the Erzurum army in April, 1829.

8. Genesis 3:22.

9. John 1:9.

1. Paul 15:54: "Engulfed is death in victory." Verses 53 to 55 read: "For this corruptible body must put on incorruption and this mortal body must put on immortality. But when this mortal body puts on immortality, then shall come to pass the word that is written: Engulfed is death in victory! O death where is thy sting?"

2. *Essays*, Vol. II, Chapter 12; Chaadaev's private library contains a copy of Montaigne's *Essays* in which the words cited above are underlined. For information on this point see Shakhovskoi's notes in *Literaturnoe nasledstvo*, Vol. 22–24 (Moscow, 1935), notes on pp. 63–64.

3. Chapter 68.

4. Plato.

5. The theory of time as memory controlled by the will was formulated by Augustine in his *Confessions*, Book 10. But Chaadaev's whole discussion of space and time is definitely post-Kantian. It represents an attempt to break from Kant's insistence that human understanding *(Verstand,* not *Vernunft,)* must operate within the limitations of space and time if it is to operate legitimately.

1. There is no work by Spinoza called *De Anima*. However, there is a text which is almost the same as the one Chaadaev cites here. It is found in Proposition 32, Part I, of Spinoza's *Ethics* under the chapter heading "De Deo." Part II of Spinoza's *Ethics* is entitled "De Mente." Since Chaadaev read the work in a German translation published in Leipzig in 1796, the mistake is understandable. See Shakhovskoi, *Literaturnoe nasledstvo*, Vol. 22–24 (Moscow, 1935), page 68, note 2.

2. Followers of the Greek philosopher Pythagoras from Samos; they tended to follow a cult which envisioned numerical relationships as the key to the rhythm of the universe.

3. Mystical and religious teachers among the Jews during the Middle Ages; through a study of biblical texts, they sometimes attempted to discover the means to achieve magical effects in nature.

4. From Spinoza, *Ethics*, Part I, Theorem 17.

5. It is true that "Newton fled," but not from London nor did he proceed to Cambridge; he actually fled from his teaching post at Cambridge itself because of the plague in 1665–1666.

6. Thomas Reid's and Dugald Stewart's philosophy of "common sense." In the post-Napoleonic era this philosophy attracted special attention in France.

7. Job. 11:12.

8. Genesis 1:26.

1. From *Paradise Regained,* Book IV, line 313. This phrase comes from Christ's answer to Satan's temptations in the desert. Satan has attempted to prove the delights of the artists and philosophers of antiquity, but Christ points out the vanity and deficiencies of the pagan philosophy with the words:

> Alas! what can they teach and not mislead,
> ignorant of themselves, of God much more,
> and how the world began, and how man fell
> degraded by himself, on grace depending?
> Much of the soul they talk, but all awry,
> and in themselves seek virtue; and to themselves
> all glory abrogate, to God give none; . . .

2. This probably refers to the position espoused by the popular scholastic textbook writer of the eighteenth century, Christian Wolff. Wolff distinguished between empirical psychology which employs the inductive method and rational psychology which utilizes the deductive method, i.e., synthesis; Chaadaev objected to this dualist approach.

3. The philosophical term is *petitio principii,* which indicates a particular weakness in a given reasoning process: in order to demonstrate a point, a principle which has not yet been proved is, nonetheless, introduced to form the basis for an entire argumentation which follows from it.

4. One might naturally expect that Chaadaev is referring to Kantian philosophy here. However, he is not. The reference is to the Scottish school of Thomas Reid, the metaphysician (1710–1796), as can be seen from the subsequent exposé and the term *empirical philosophy.* Reid opposed the introduction of mathematical formulae into meta-

physical or moral formulae. He also aimed at refuting Hume's skeptical epistemological theory. Reid affirmed the impossibility of proving the existence of the external world from reason or from experience; instead he introduced the doctrine of an original instinct or "common sense" as the basis for his reflections on nature.

5. The philosophy of Victor Cousin (1792–1867), who lectured at the Sorbonne from 1815 to 1817 and again from 1828 until his retirement in 1851. He combined the doctrines of Thomas Reid and Dugald Stewart with those of Frederick W. J. von Schelling. In the preface to his *Fragments philosophiques,* Cousin wrote down several ideas which are strikingly close to those of Chaadaev: "*la raison est à la lettre une révelation, une révelation nécessaire et universelle, qui n'a manqué à aucun homme et a eclairé tout homme à sa venue en ce monde; la raison est la médiatrice nécessaire entre Dieu et l'homme, ce logos de Pythagore et de Platon, ce verbe fait chair qui sert d'interprète à Dieu et de précepteur à l'homme, homme à la fois et Dieu tout ensemble.*"

6. Shakhovskoi states that Schelling himself called his system "transcendental idealism," and that Chaadaev thus called Schelling's philosophy by that name, but that Chaadaev made a mistake here by writing "transcendent" instead of "transcendental." See *Literaturnoe nasledstvo,* Vol. 22–24 (Moscow, 1935), p. 72, note 6. However, Falk (*Das Weltbild Peter J. Tschaadajews nach seinen acht "Philosophischen Briefen"* [Munich, 1954]) claims that it is possible that Chaadaev really meant to use the word "transcendent" instead of "transcendental" here. Falk's reasoning is the following: It is true that Schelling had termed his system "transcendental" idealism in his book "*System des transcendental Idealismus* (Tübingen, 1800).

But Chaadaev favored the later Schelling who attempted to overcome the pantheistic elements in his philosophy by forming a "positive" philosophy of revelation. In studying Chaadaev's personal letters to Schelling, it appears that Falk's interpretation outweighs that of Shakhovskoi.

7. *Pensées et opuscules* (Paris, 1946), p. 80. The exact quotation reads " . . . *toute la suite des hommes pendant la cours de tant de siècles doit être considérée comme un même homme qui subsiste toujours et qui apprend continuellement . . . . .*" Chaadaev incorrectly cites Pascal as having written: "*toute la suite des hommes est un seul homme qui existe toujours . . . . *" Both Shakhovskoi (*Lit. nasled.*, p. 61 and p. 74), and Falk (*Das Weltbild*, p. 116) have pointed out the difference between Chaadaev's interpretation and Pascal's actual meaning in this case. In Chaadaev's library Shakhovskoi noted Rio's book *Essai sur l'esprit humain dans l'antiquité*, which begins with the citation above; therefore, it seems likely that Chaadaev was incorrectly quoting not from Pascal directly but from Rio's work.

8. Chaadaev's assumption here is not borne out by the history of mediaeval philosophy. Many mediaeval philosophers between Anselm and Descartes utilized this so-called "ontological proof" for God's existence.

9. *De Legibus,* Book I, sections 26 and 27.

10. The rationalism of Descartes and his followers.

11. The philosophy of the empiricists, such as Locke and Condillac.

12. *Méditations métaphysiques,* Part I, "*Méditations touchant la première philosophie*" (Paris, 1932), p. 83. At the very beginning of the third meditation are the words "*Je fermerai maintenant les yeux, je boucherai mes oreilles, je détournerai tous mes sens, j'effacerai même de ma*

pensée toutes les images des choses corporelles . . . . "

13. Professor Buhle had influenced Chaadaev towards Kantianism during his youth. The reference here is clearly to the Königsberg philosopher himself. Chaadaev has a copy of Kant's *Kritik der reinen Vernunft* and the *Kritik der praktischen Vernunft* in his private library. He wrote many comments in the margins of Kant's books; see the reproductions in *Lit. nasled.,* p. 15 and p. 73. Chaadaev crossed out the title of Kant's *Critique of Pure Reason* and wrote over it *Critique of Adamite Reason.* Chaadaev disagreed with Kant's approach to reason; he felt that Kant has erroneously begun with "Adamite" reason, i.e., human reason after Adam's sin, hence "fallen" reason. According to Chaadaev, Kant should have tried to construct absolute reason, reason before the Fall of Adam, i.e., a truly "pure" reason.

14. The philosophy of Fichte.

15. On the back of the title page of Kant's *Critique of Practical Reason,* Chaadaev wrote eight verses from the gospel of St. John: "He was not the light . . ."; *Lit nasled.,* p. 71. In the Bible these words refer to John the Baptist. It appears that Chaadaev was attempting to indicate that, just as John the Baptist was only the forerunner of the true light, so Kant was merely a forerunner of a superior philosophy of the future.

1. The quotation is exact; it is from Voltaire's *Essai sur les moeurs,* Vol. IV; *Oeuvres Complètes,* Vol. XIX, de l'imprimerie de la société littéraire-typographique (no place of publication given, 1784). Voltaire's text goes on after the paragraph cited by Chaadaev to the following explanation:

> *Il faut que notre patrie de l'Europe ait eu dans ses moeurs et dans son génie un caractère qui ne se trouve ni dans la Thrace où les Turcs ont établi le siège de leur empire, ni dans la Tartarie dont ils sortirent autrefois. Trois choses influent sans cesse sur l'esprit des hommes, le climat, le gouvernement et la religion: c'est la seule manière d'expliquer l'énigme de ce monde.* [p. 352]

The entire passage refers to the period of the Renaissance which Voltaire places in late fifteenth and early sixteenth-century Italy. In Volume III of his *Essai sur les moeurs* Voltaire addresses himself to this same point:

> *La nature produit alors des hommes extraordinaires presqu'en tous les genres, surtout en Italie. Ce qui frappe encore dans ce siècle illustre, c'est que malgré les guerres que l'ambition excita, et malgré les querelles de religion qui commençaient à troubler les Etats, ce même génie qui fesait fleurir les beaux arts à Rome, à Naples, à Florence, à Venise, á Ferrare, et qui de là portait la lumière dans l'Europe, adoucit d'abord les moeurs des hommes dans presque toutes les provinces de l'Europe chrétienne.* [p. 56].

2. The eighteenth-century Rationalist approach to history, in particular, that of Voltaire.

3. Newton's law.

4. Eighteenth-century Rationalism.

5. Aristotle, who was born in 382 B. C. in Stagira, a city

on the Thracian peninsula of Chalcidice. Aristotle was often called "the Stagirite."

6. François Fénelon (1651–1715) was the gifted preacher admitted to the Académie française in 1693. His conversion to quietism led to eventual disgrace and ruin; Fénelon's *Dialogues sur l'éloquence,* composed in 1686 but published posthumously in 1718, contained the thesis that the communion of the soul with God rendered the practice of any religious rites needless. Here Chaadaev is probably referring to Fénelon's admiration for Homer's works which served as the basis for Fénelon's most famous book, *Télémaque,* published in Paris in 1699.

7. The prophet Daniel; see especially 2 Daniel, 7: 1–24.

8. The birth of Christ and the coming of Christianity.

9. The Roman empire.

10. In Volume IV of his *Essai sur les moeurs,* Voltaire wrote: *"L'opinion n'a causé de guerres civiles que chez les chrétiens"* (p. 379).

11. Matthew 6:33.

12. The eighteenth-century Rationalist School, and probably the works of Voltaire in particular.

13. François Guizot lectured as a professor of history at the Sorbonne in 1812. In 1823 he published his *Essais sur l'histoire de France.* Chaadaev was in Paris during the winter of 1823–1824. In 1825 Guizot published his *Mémoires relatifs à la Révolution d'Angleterre;* in 1826, *l'Histoire de Charles Ier;* in 1828, *Histoire générale de la civilisation en Europe depuis la chute de l'empire romain jusqu'à la Révolution française;* in 1829, Volumes I, II, and III of his *Histoire de la civilisation en France depuis la chute de l'empire romain jusqu'en 1789.* See Charles Quénet, *Tchaadaev et les lettres philosophiques* (Paris,

1931), pp. 149–155, for an exact analysis of the extent of Guizot's influence upon Chaadaev.

14. Followers of Peter Waldo, a rich merchant from Lyons who in the twelfth century preached the gospel with an anti-sacerdotal interpretation of it. The Waldensians were active missionaries and spread their faith from Spain to Bohemia.

15. This refers to Calvin and his role in the condemnation of Michael Servetus (properly Miguel Servète), the Spanish scholar (1511–1553). Servète published several books on theology in which he held rather unorthodox views. On his way to Naples Servète was apprehended by the magistrates of Geneva on a charge of blasphemy and heresy. Calvin was extremely influential in securing Servète's condemnation to death. Since Servète refused to recant, he was burned in Geneva in 1553.

16. Huldreich Zwingli (1484–1531), a Catholic priest who denounced the supremacy of the pope, upheld the Bible as the guide to faith and morals, and held that the Eucharist was only a memorial service.

17. Thomas Cranmer (1489–1556) had been Henry VIII's chaplain and his enthusiastic supporter. In 1553 Cranmer became Archbishop of Canterbury. The book of prayers edited under his auspices became a favorite in the Anglican Church.

18. John 17:11.

1. See Letter V, explanatory note 7, for this paraphrase of Pascal's words.

2. Edward Gibbon's *Decline and Fall of the Roman Empire.*

3. Chaadaev was with the victorious Russian army when it marched into Paris on April 1, 1814. Napoleon had gathered an incredible collection of Greek statues and especially Roman copies of Greek works during his conquests; he had had them brought to Paris. These are the works of art to which Chaadaev is referring here.

4. Chaadaev traveled again in western Europe, from 1823 to 1826.

5. Eighteenth-century Rationalism, especially Voltaire's work on history.

6. Arnold Herman Heeren (1760–1842) was a noted German historian of Greek studies. He became professor of history at Göttingen in 1801. His most famous works were *Geschichte des Studiums der Klassischen Literatur seit dem Wiederaufleben der Wissenschaften* (Göttingen, 1792–1802) and *Geschichte des europäischen Staatensystems und seiner Kolonien* (Göttingen, 1809).

7. Georg Frederich Creuzer—Chaadaev's spelling, "Kreutzer," is erroneous in this case—(1771–1858) was a noted German scholar, whose works on Greek religion were influential in his day. In 1804 Creuzer became professor of philology and ancient history at Heidelberg. The period from 1815 to 1850 was the high point in his scholarly career. His chief works were *Die historische Kunst der Griechen* (Leipzig and Darmstadt, 1848) and especially his *Symbolik und Mythologie der alten Volker, besonders der Griechen* (Leipzig and Darmstadt, 1st edition 1810–

1812; 2nd edition 1819–1823, and 3rd edition 1836–1843, in four volumes). Chaadaev is probably referring to the first or second edition of this particular work.

8. In Greek mythology Typhon was a giant, the son of Tartarus and Gaea. He had a hundred heads shaped like those of a serpent, and flames darted from his many mouths and eyes. Typhon made war on heaven, but Zeus wounded him, cast Mount Etna upon his head, and finally buried the rest of his body in the earth. The imprisoned giant still belches forth his fire from Mount Etna and groans thunderously.

9. Ahriman was the devil of ancient Zoroastrianism; he was the chief spirit and source of all evil.

1. The critical attitude of the eighteenth-century philosophers vis-à-vis the Middle Ages.

2. The Romantic Idealists of the early nineteenth century. Chaadaev's emphasis on the necessity of creating proper material conditions for intellectual activity is a constant theme in the letters.

3. This refers to the Reformation and post-Reformation period.

4. Roman Catholicism and the Papacy.

5. The Protestant Reformation.

6. Roman Catholicism in western Europe.

EXPLANATORY NOTES
TO THE APOLOGIA OF A MADMAN

1. I Corinthians 13:4–7: "Charity is patient; charity does not envy, is not pretentious, is not puffed up, is not ambitious, is not self-seeking, is not provoked; thinks no evil, does not rejoice over wickedness, but rejoices with the truth; bears all things, believes all things, endures all things."

2. This refers to the publication of "The First Philosophical Letter" and the reaction against it.

3. The religious and political writer Hugues Félicité Robert de Lamennais (1782–1854). His works *Essai sur l'indifférence en matière de religion* and *Défense de l'Essai sur l'indifférence en matière de religion* were both found in Chaadaev's private library; see Shakhovskoi, *Literaturnoe Nasledstvo*, Vol. 22–24, (Moscow, 1935), p. 71. Shakhovskoi also states that in a text of the *Apologia of a Madman* which was in the hands of Chernyshevsky the phrase "a great writer of our time" was footnoted specifically as referring to Lamennais.

The first two parts of Lamennais's *Essai sur l'indifférence en matière de religion* are important to an understanding of Chaadaev's own position. Chaadaev had underlined several words in the book and had made marginal notes, as well. The final note is dated December 1, 1829, and that is the very date at the end of "The First Philosophical Letter." Shakhovskoi holds that the influence of Lamennais upon Chaadaev was much stronger than that of Ballanche, de Bonald, or de Maistre (p. 71).

Lamennais wrote several essays in Chateaubriand's *Conservateur* from 1817 to 1823, but the monarchical tendencies of Villele finally alienated him from that group.

252

During 1830 and 1831 Lamennais published his liberal Catholic journal *L'Avenir* with the dedication "Dieu and Liberté." In 1831 he was called to Rome by Gregory XVI. In this case the pope was strongly influenced by temporal authorities; he suppressed Lamennais and his movement because of the dangerously "liberal" tendencies within *L'Avenir*. Much to Lamennais's own surprise, he received an extremely cold reception in Rome. In 1832 the encyclical *Mirari Vos* denounced Lamennais's *L'Avenir*. Lamennais replied with his *Les Paroles d'un croyant* which definitely marked his break with Rome. Gregory answered with another encyclical, *Singulari Nos*, in 1834. Lamennais continued to write numerous articles and books. He actively supported the revolution in 1848. Chaadaev wrote the *Apologia of a Madman* in 1837; but by that time he had apparently become disenchanted with Lamennais's tendency to identify himself with the popular, democratic movement in France.

4. Chaadaev detected a Russian tendency to have contact with western Europe and to submit to that cultural influence as early as the middle of the sixteenth century.

5. Peter the Great.

6. This is aimed not only at some of those later intellectuals known as Slavophiles but also at the group known as the "Official Nationalists," especially the coterie around Pogodin, Polevoi, Gretch, Weltmann, Burachek, and Shevyrev. In general Chaadaev is attacking all the nationalistic, isolationist groups in Russia.

7. See the above note.

8. Bayer, Schiller, Miller, and especially Schloezer. Gerhard Friederich Muller (1705–1783), the successor to Gotlieb Bayer, was a prodigious researcher in Russia. He ransacked archives in Siberia, found source materials on the

Time of the Troubles, for example, charters issued by Boris Godunov and Vasili Shuisky. Muller's book *Sammlung russischer Geschichte* (St. Petersburg, 1732) aroused the curiosity of the famous German historian August-Ludwig von Schloezer (1735–1790). Schloezer came to St. Petersburg in 1761 as a professor and became a member of the Academy of Sciences. There he worked on Russian chronicles. He left Russia in 1776 to become professor of history at the University of Göttingen. His famous *Probe russischer Annalen* (Bremen and Göttingen, 1768) was the first effort at applying a critical method to the study of Russian chronicles.

9. The noted Russian historian Nikolai Karamzin (1776–1826), whom Pushkin called "the Columbus of Russian history," made Russian history popular and appealing to his literary generation with his famous work, *The History of the Russian State* (St. Petersburg, 1816–1826). Chaadaev had known Karamzin personally since his days in St. Petersburg in 1816.

10. Probably the writings of Nikolai Polevoi (1796–1846) and Mikhail Pogodin (1800–1875). Polevoi attempted to write a national history, *A History of the Russian People* in six volumes from 1830 to 1833 (an obvious antithesis to Karamzin's *History of the Russian State*). Although Polevoi had considerable journalistic talent, he possessed none of the literary talents or refinements of a Karamzin. For this reason, Chaadaev considered Polevoi's work to be second-rate. Polevoi's task appears in reality to have been beyond his basic intellectual capabilities. Mikhail Pogodin became a lecturer at Moscow University in 1835 in place of his teacher, M. T. Kachenovski, who had taught Chaadaev. Pogodin edited the *Moscow Messenger* from 1827 to 1830. In general, his popular writings contained a

254

highly nationalistic interpretation of Russian history and later he himself became one of the staunchest supporters of tsarist imperialism.

11. The Time of the Troubles, from 1598 to 1613. The last male heir of the original Riurik dynasty, Fedor Ivanovich, died in 1598. Boris Godunov became tsar upon election by the Zemski Sobor, but he was faced with years of famine and pestilence on the land, plus a contender for the throne, the so-called False Dmitri. This pretender to the throne claimed that one of the sons of Ivan IV, Dmitri, had not died in 1591 and that he was the true Dmitri, rightful heir to the throne. With the help of Polish soldiers Dmitri seized the throne in 1605 to reign until 1606. The boyar, Vasili Shuisky, then seized the throne and held onto it until 1610. 1611 was the nadir of Russian power; the Poles occupied the Kremlin, the Swedes invaded northern Russia, and several other pretenders to the throne arose throughout Russia. A nationalist movement, inspired by the orthodox monks at Trinity monastery and supported by the lesser gentry and lower classes, led by Pozharski and Minin, threw out the foreign intruders. In 1613 Mikhail Romanov was elected tsar to begin the long Romanov dynasty in Russia. Chaadaev considered the Time of the Troubles to be an extremely important period in Russian history; in his mind, it was one of the rare times in which the "people," the Russian nation, acted as a real force in history.

12. *The Philosophical Letters Addressed to a Lady.*

13. "The First Philosophical Letter."

14. "The First Philosophical Letter."

15. Nikolai Gogol's play *Revizor* (*The Inspector General*). In 1824, scenes 7, 8, 9, and 10 were presented in St. Petersburg; on June 16/28, 1830, parts of it were played

again, then the third act was performed in Moscow. Finally most of the play with a few lines cut out was performed in Moscow. Here Chaadaev might be referring specifically to the performance in Moscow on December 2/14, 1835, which he could have attended. The "almost tragic emotion" resulted from Gogol's satire of the corruption and bribery which existed in Russian provincial life.

Index

A

Academicians (Greece), 179
Ahriman, 184, 250
Alekseev, Nikolai, 228
Alexander I, 3, 6, 38, 223, 235
Alexander the Great, 140, 145
Anselm, 112 n, 244
Anthony, Saint, 62
Apologia of a Madman, vii–ix, 2, 9, 17–18, 253
Aristotle, 60, 134, 180, 191, 246
Augustine, 240

B

Bacon, Francis, 77, 95, 178
Ballanche, Pierre-Simon, 252
Basil, Saint, 55
Bayer, Gottlieb, 253
Benckendorf, Count Alexander, 224–225
Boldyrev, A. V., 226
Bonald, Louis de, 229, 252
Buhle, Gottlieb von, 4, 245

C

Cabalists, 90, 241
Caesar, Julius, 185
Calvin, Jean, 158, 248
Cato, 134
Chaadaev, Peter Yakovlevich, vii–ix, xiii, xiv
biography, 1–11
on democracy, 201
"insanity" of, 225
on nationalism, 135, 199–200, 212–213
philosophy of history, 13–19, 128–153, 205–208, 214–217
as a revolutionary or reactionary, 228–231
on Russia and Europe, 27–51, 187–188, 199–205, 208–214
on serfdom, 60–61
on time and space, 82–84
as Westernizer or Slavophile, 17
Chateaubriand, François René de, 252
China, 144, 151, 152
Christianity, 40–50, 73–74, 107, 129, 132, 139
Byzantine and Kievan, 15–16
intellectual character of, 191–198
and paganism of Greece and Rome, 166 n–167 n, 168, 184–186
schism, 39
and slavery, 60–61
superiority to other reli-

gions, 141–152
unity, xiv, 13, 18, 157–161
see also Protestantism,
Reformation, Roman
Catholicism
Chrysostom, St. John, 54
Cicero, 31, 112, 178
Condillac, Étienne de, 244
Cousin, Victor, 137, 243
Cranmer, Thomas, 158, 248
Creuzer, Georg Frederich,
184 n, 249

D
David, 134, 175–176
Decembrists, xiii, 4, 6, 38,
226, 235
Democritus, 178
Descartes, René, 95, 112 n,
120, 122, 244

E
Egypt, 145, 150
Epicurus, 134, 177–179

F
Falk, Heinrich, 221, 230,
243–244
Fénelon, François, 137, 247
Fichte, Johann Gottlieb, 4,
121, 245
Florovski, Georgi, 230
Frederick the Great, 144

G
Gershenzon, M. O., 222, 229,
231
Gibbon, Edward, 167, 249
Godunov, Boris, 61, 239, 254

Gogol, Nikolai (*Revizor*),
217, 218, 255–256
Golitsyn, Prince D. M., 224
Granovsky, T. N., 9
Greece, 137, 145, 152
art, 167–169, 184 n
Gregory of Nazianzus, 55
Gregory of Tours, 166 n
Griboedov, Alexander (*Woe
from Wit*), 4, 5
Guizot, François, 14, 154 n,
236, 247–248

H
Heeren, Arnold, 184 n, 249
Hegelian argument, 9
Henry VIII, 46, 158, 248
Herodotus, 130, 150, 166 n
Herzen, A. I., xiii, 9, 16, 226,
228
Hipparchus, 130
history, 39–40, 139–143, 145
philosophy of, 14, 124–153,
162–188, 205–208
see also Chaadaev, Russia
Homer, 134, 183–187, 247
Hume, David, 243

I
idealism (German transcendental), 109–110, 192,
243–244, 251
India, 144, 150
Islam, 180–183

J
John, Saint, 159, 245, 248
Julian, 140

K

Kachenovski, M. T., 4, 254
Kant, Immanuel, 4, 120–122, 240, 242, 245
Karamzin, Nikolai, 17, 211, 232, 254
Kepler, Johannes, 96 n, 130
Khomyakov, A. S., 10
Koyré, Alexander, 230, 231

L

Lagides, 140, 145
Lamennais, Huques Félicité Robert de, 201, 252–253
Leo X, 155
Locke, John, 244
Longinov, M. N., 221, 223
Luther, Martin, 154
Lyubomudrye, 232

M

Maistre, Joseph de, 229
Marcus, Aurelius, 134, 140, 176
Maxim of Tyr, 184 n
Milton, John, 105, 242
Milyukov, P. N., 229
Mohammed, 134, 180–183
Montaigne, Michel de, 74, 240
Moses, 133, 170–176, 224
Moskovski Nablyudatel, 8
Muller, Gerhard Friederich, 253
Muraviev, Nikita, 4
Muraviev-Apostol brothers, 5

N

Nadezhdin, N. I., 8, 226

Napoleon I, 4, 144, 235
Necropolis (Moscow), 51
Newton, Isaac, 93, 95–97, 130, 241, 246
Nicholas I, 1, 10, 15, 224, 226

O

Obleukhov, D. A., 231
Odoevsky, V. F., xiii, 232
Official Nationalism, 15, 232, 253

P

Panova, Ekaterina D., 7, 233–234
Pascal, Blaise, 110, 163, 244, 249
Paul I, 3
Paul, Saint, 72, 199, 240
Pericles, 145
Peter the Great, 3, 16, 17, 18, 38, 202–205, 209, 213, 217, 235, 253
Philosophical Letters Addressed to a Lady, vii–ix, xiv, 2, 212
"First Philosophical Letter," 1, 7–9, 18, 199, 212, 216, 225, 226, 233–252
philosophy, 105–123
and science, 89–100
moral, 62–71, 79–82, 86–87, 100–104, 135–136, 197
see also Christianity, history, idealism, rationalism
Photius, 39 n, 235
Plato, 54, 71, 82
"archetypes," 122

on Homer, 134
Phaedrus, 238
sensuality of, 137, 168
Symposium, 176 n
Plekhanov, Georgii, 228
Plutarch, 183 n
Pogodin, M. P., 232, 253, 254
Polevoi, Nikolai, 253, 254
Protestantism, 153–156, 158
Pushkin, Alexander, 5, 7, 223
Pythagoras, 71, 90, 168, 241, 243

Q
Quénet, Charles, 221, 229–230

R
Radishchev, Alexander, 3
rationalism, 74–79, 111–123
of Enlightenment, 45, 130–132, 174, 191, 236, 249
Reformation, 157–159
Reid, Thomas, 101, 241, 242–243
Riasanovsky, Nicholas, 232
Roman Catholicism, 13, 17, 40–50, 156–161, 192–198
Rome, 150, 166 n–167 n
Russia,
and Europe, 27–51, 187–188
place in history, ix–x, 15–19, 199–212
uniqueness, 213–218

S
Saint-Simon, Claude Henri, 224

Samarin, Yuri F., 9
Scheibert, Peter, 230
Schelling, Friedrich William, xiii, 4, 137, 243–244
Schleiermacher, Friedrich, 137
Schloezer, August von (historian), 4, 253, 254
Schloezer, Christian von (professor of philosophy), 4
Scholastics (medieval), 180
Seleucides, 140
Semenovsky regiment, 4
Semenovsky uprising of 1820, 4–6
serfdom, 60–61
Servetus, Michael, 248
Shakhovskoi, D. I., ix, 222, 230, 243–244
Shcherbatov, Ivan (cousin of Chaadaev), 4
Shcherbatov, M. M. (grandfather of Chaadaev), 2
Shcherbatov, Mikhail (uncle of Chaadaev), 4
Shcherbatova, Anna M. (aunt of Chaadaev), 2, 223
Shevyrev, S. P., 10, 232, 253
Shkurinov, P. S., 221, 229
Shuisky, Prince Vasily, 61, 239, 254
Slavophiles, xiii, 9, 16–19, 206, 208–209, 253
Socrates, 71, 133, 176–177
Spinoza, Benedict, 89, 91, 241
Stewart, Dugald, 101, 241, 243

Stoics, 178–179
Sverbeev, D. N., 221

T
Tacitus, 185
Tasso, Torquato, 43, 236
Telescope, 1–2, 8, 225, 226
Titus-Livy, 166 n
Turgenev, Nikolai, 4, 5
Typhon, 184, 250

V
Vasilchikov, Prince I. V., 5, 6
Villele, 252
Voltaire, François Marie

Arouet de, 124, 142, 236, 246, 247

W
Waldensians (followers of Peter Waldo), 154, 248
Westernizers, xiii, 9, 16–19
Wolff, Christian, 242

Y
Yakushkin, Ivan, 4, 5

Z
Zhikharev, Mikhail, 4, 222
Zhukovsky, V. A., 9
Zoroaster, 71
Zwingli, Huldreich, 158, 248